TABLE OF CONTENTS

CHAPTER 1:
SECRET #1 YOUR PURPOSE WITH FIRE

"I used to think freedom meant doing whatever you want. It means knowing who you are, what you are supposed to be doing on this earth, and then simply doing it." ~Natalie Goldberg

THE REALITY IS THAT WE ALL have the same amount of time in a day.

We can choose to do with it what we will. The other reality is that there are so many things we need to do or that we could do that we can often feel pulled in a million different directions. We can be distracted by the chaos of life and begin to forget what we really want to accomplish and what it is that is most important to us.

Life can begin to feel like we are just moving from one thing on our massive "to do" list to the next. We bypass our family members in the hallways of our home, barely noticing them as we rush through our day. Living this way feels tiring, frustrating, and disconnecting. We are stuck in a pattern of going through the motions, and we are left with a dimmed sense of excitement for life and our purpose in it.

Since you are reading this book, please take what I am about to say with the love that I intend. This is your wake-up call.

Right here, right now. Listen, I know you are busy, so I am just going to get right to the point. You are being called to do something great. You have a divine purpose in this life, something that only you have to give to your family, your community, to the world. You have been given gifts and talents to help the people around you.

I know your life is busy, and there are many things that can distract you from your purpose, but I need you to stay focused. The world needs you to stay focused. You need to stay focused because living your purpose is one of the most important things you will ever do.

Bronnie Ware, the author of *The Top 5 Regrets of the Dying*, helped us understand just how important living your purpose is.[2] She interviewed dozens of terminally ill patients in hospice care and asked them about their deepest regrets. The number one regret was, "I wish I had the courage to live a life that was truer to myself, not the life others expected of me."

Right here, right now, you need to have the courage to step toward a life that is true to yourself and the purpose that you were put on this earth to do.

I know at this moment you might be thinking that you don't have time for one more thing. You are likely working way too many hours at work or in your business; you are juggling family life and all the craziness that involves and are just struggling to stay afloat. I used to feel like that. I used to feel like I didn't have time to do one more thing.

At that point in my life, I didn't understand what doing that one thing would do for me. I didn't understand that the thing I was being called to do was divinely inspired. I didn't know that I wouldn't be doing it alone, that if I just started, I would get a lot of help from the universe. I didn't realize that when I began to live my purpose, my life would get easier instead of harder. That I would have more energy, would be lifted and strengthened and would feel more joy than I could have imagined. I didn't understand that the universe had set up a system to help me win at living my purpose and that I didn't have to do it all right now. I couldn't see that I just needed to take the very next step and then the very next step after that.

I promise that the same is true for you. You just need to take the very next step toward living your purpose. You don't need to see the whole picture; you don't need to see how it will all work out or how you will fit it into your busy schedule.

You just need to have an open heart and a willingness to take the very next step. To open your mind to the possibility that there is more for you in this life and that you are being called to do something great. Is this your wake-up call from the universe? I believe it is. All you need to do is have the courage to take the very next small step forward.

If you would like support with finding the missing spark for igniting your purpose-driven life, you can claim your free spot in the My Fire Within Class at
www.myfirewithin.com/resources.

Fire Principles Revealed

Have you ever had the feeling that there is more going on in this life than what appears to be, a sense that there really is a higher power? I've had this feeling all my life. That feeling took me on a journey in search of answers to my big questions of *why am I here, and what am I supposed to be doing*?

My search took me to the faraway land of Indonesia, to spiritual books, churches, and even to sweat lodges. Along the way, I found evidence of a higher power that I could not deny. And yet, I did not have a complete picture of what this life is really about.

That is until I learned a key understanding that made all the puzzle pieces fit together. This knowledge answered my big questions and pointed me in the direction of understanding the plan that the universe has for me and how I could work within that plan to create the life I longed for as well as live my purpose. So, what principle did I learn that created such an earth-shattering collaboration with the universe?

The knowledge that helped me become a partner with the Creator was discovering Fire Principles.

What are Fire Principles, you might ask?

Fire Principles are very real and tangible. They are a set of laws outlined by the Creator, that when we align to a Fire Principle, gives us an alternate result. What I mean is that when we want a result, we need to take any action that is seemingly unrelated but will create the result we want. That works upon a paradox. It's a pendulum.

When you take a long necklace with a pendulum on the bottom and swing it, you complete an action on one side by drawing up the pendulum and then releasing it. What happens next? It swings, right? The action that you take on the one hand creates an alternate response as the pendulum swings up the other side. It's counterintuitive. If you want the pendulum to go to the left, can't you simply push the pendulum to the left? You can, but it's not sustainable because the moment you let go, it's going to swing to the right.

To go in the direction we want to go, we need to take action in what seems unrelated. To create the results we want, we must take the action that is in alignment with the Fire Principle that corresponds with the result we want.

To understand how this works, let's look at the bees. According to the BBC, one-third of all the food we eat is dependent on the bees.[3] This is because when bees collect nectar from flowers, they inadvertently transfer pollen from one flower to another. This pollination is vital in the flowering plant reproducing. This means that the food we eat from crops like apples, almonds, and so many others, rely on the bees. Without the bees, we wouldn't have these crops, and we wouldn't have the foods we need to survive. The bees are literally saving our lives.

So what do the bees have to do with Fire Principles? When the bee wakes up in the morning and wants to collect yummy nectar, it is not thinking; *I am going to save all the humans today by pollinating their crops.* It is just going for the nectar, and in the process, the bees are saving the world. The bees take action and get a life-changing and seemingly unrelated result.

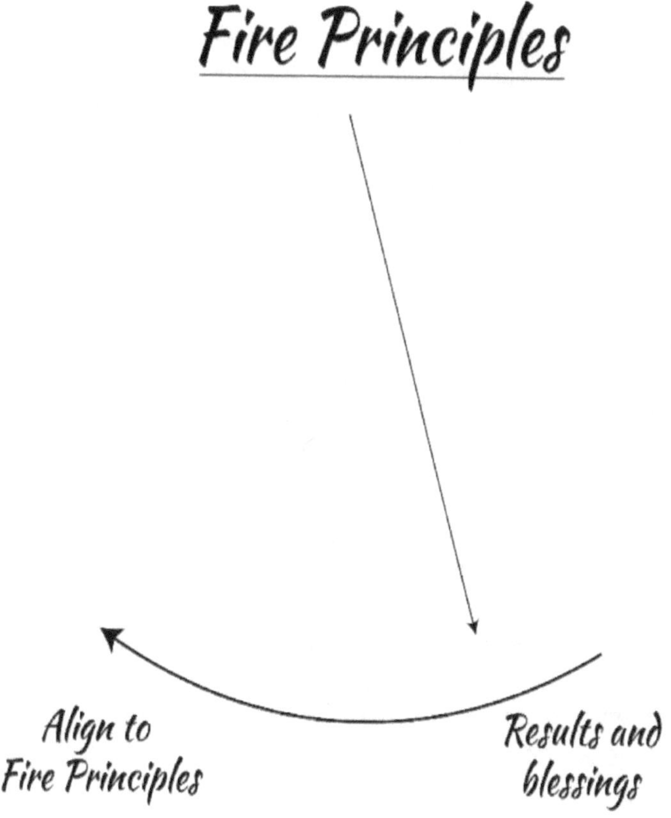

Now, let's look at how Fire Principles work in the lives of people. One example of how these principles work is that people who are constantly looking for love and asking themselves if they are happy will not be happy.

People who are looking outside themselves and trying to serve others out of pure love are happy. That's why I use the analogy of the pendulum. We cannot find happiness through an inward search for happiness. Finding happiness requires us to do the opposite and look outward to serve those around us.

As Mahatma Gandhi so eloquently put it, "The best way to find yourself is to lose yourself in the service of others."

I have sometimes struggled with truly understanding what the Fire Principles are and how they affect me. Stephen Covey explains, "The fundamental idea is that there are principles that govern human effectiveness —natural laws in the human dimension that are just as real, just as unchanging and arguably 'there' as laws such as gravity are in the physical dimension."

This quote helped me to understand that in this world of relativism, there are Fire Principles that are real, and are there to help us step into our potential.

Before knowing about Fire Principles, I lived a life of what I thought was freedom, where I could do whatever I wanted, and I was only accountable to myself. This led to heartache and regret. I thought I had freedom, but I was unknowingly shackled by my poor decisions as I smashed against Fire Principles that I didn't know existed.

Once my eyes were opened to the Fire Principles, I found real freedom. As I turned to my Creator for guidance, I was lifted, strengthened, and empowered more than I had ever been before. I wanted to follow his Fire Principles because they helped me feel joy and get closer to the people I love. They helped me to become more of the person I want to be.

We cannot change Fire Principles because they are not in style or convenient or even socially preferred. As Cecil B. DeMille said, "It is impossible for us to break the law. We can only break ourselves against the law."

This was important for me to understand because I spent so many years of my life not understanding why life was so hard.

When I learned about the Fire Principles, it was as though I could see clearly and recognize that I was breaking myself when I went against the laws. When I began to align my life to the Fire Principles, I felt more joy and more connected to the people I love. I felt more connected to my Creator and began to create the life I have always wanted.

When we align with our Creator's laws, we receive the attached result or blessing for that law. As we give up our short-term comfort and desires to align with Fire Principles, we receive far greater than we give. And we become changed in the process. Our character grows, our capacity increases, and we step into our divine potential.

We cannot build the spiritual muscles of the soul by sitting on the couch of mediocrity. I promise that learning about Fire Principles is one of the most important undertakings in this life. What an adventure life becomes when our spiritual eyes are opened, and we can see things as they really are.

Now that you know there are Fire Principles, you might be wondering *what are Fire Principles?* After all, you can't align with them if you don't know what they are.

Digging Deep

Do you feel like you are living your purpose?

Do you know how to receive inspiration from the Creator to guide you in living your purpose?

How important is it to you to learn how to receive inspiration from the Creator so you can live a purposeful and passionate life?

CHAPTER 2:
FOUR PRIMARY LAWS OF FIRE

"The day came when the risk to remain tight in a bud was more painful than the risk it took to blossom." ~Anais Nin

I REMEMBER WHEN I FIRST started learning about Fire Principles.

My mentor, Brandon, was telling me all about them, and I was so excited that these Fire Principles existed that I wanted to know all of them immediately! I wanted him to give me a list so I could start following them. After all, I needed all the help I could get in every area of my life!

What I didn't realize, however, is that certain Fire Principles are more important than others and that I actually wasn't supposed to learn them all at once. I was supposed to learn them one at a time. *So, which of the Fire Principles were the most important,* I wondered? *Which ones did I need to know first?*

I had heard about the Law of Attraction, and I wondered if that was one of the most important Fire Principles. I will never forget the moment when Brandon revealed the truth about the Law of Attraction and why some people get no results by following that law alone.

He explained that the law of attraction is not one of the most important Fire Principles and that there are, in fact, four Fire Principles that make up what I call the Four Primary Laws of Fire. The Four Primary Laws of Fire are composed of the Fire Principles that ignite the fire within us. As he revealed the Four Primary Laws of Fire, I understood why they were even more important than the Law of Attraction, which is one of the Fire Principles but not the most important one. And I could clearly see why the Four Primary Laws of Fire are critical in getting the results we want.

Although I wish I could give you all the Fire Principles, I know that I can't cover them all in the pages of this book. I learned them over time and one by one. I will, however, share with you what I can. For instance, I know that the Four Primary Laws of Fire are the most important ones for you in order for you to know to get results in the areas of living your purpose, prosperity, and having passionate relationships. These are critical in lighting the fire within us so we can light up ourselves, our families, our community, and the world.

The order of priority of the Four Primary Laws of Fire are:

1. Alignment to Fire Principles
2. State
3. Service
4. Growth

Now that you know what the Four Primary Laws of Fire do, let's dive in deeper to help you understand how aligning with them will help you get what you want in life.

Digging Deep

What does true success mean to you? What does success look like in the areas of health, wealth, relationships, and service?

CHAPTER 3:
PRIMARY LAW OF FIRE – STATE OF MIND

"You've always had the power, my dear. You just had to learn it for yourself." ~The Wizard of Oz

I REMEMBER VIVIDLY GOING THROUGH LIFE feeling like something was wrong with me because I did not feel in control of my emotions.

I am a fairly passionate person, and although this passion brings many blessings, it also requires me to be able to control my temper so I can be the person I want to be. I recall feeling the massive ups and downs of my emotions. They seemed to turn on a dime depending on the circumstances I was facing at any given moment.

If things were going my way, I felt happy and excited. If things did not work out, I felt disappointment, frustration, and anger. The funny thing is that when I think back to that point in my life, it didn't actually matter what circumstances I was going through, what truly mattered was the meaning I gave to the situation and how I chose to feel about it.

What do I mean? Simply that, sometimes, I could experience the very same situation but would feel completely differently about it, depending on the meaning I assigned the situation at any given time.

As I'm writing this book, I'm thinking back to one time when my daughter, Zoe, was acting out, and she hit me. I wanted her to be respectful and felt exasperated and frustrated when she lashed out at me. As much as I hate to admit it, I started asking myself questions like *why is she such a brat?* Another time, Zoe was acting out with the same behavior, but that time, I was not angry or frustrated with her. I was able to give her consequences in a loving way and feel compassion toward her.

What was different? How could I feel and respond in a completely different way when the situations were the same? Why is it that we can, at times, get through challenging experiences and still have compassion, love faith, and hope, while at other times, small circumstances seem crushing?

I struggled for years, trying to figure that question out. I wondered how I could be more loving with my husband and my children and how I could be more of the person I wanted to be, even when going through stressful circumstances.

I know that this life has ups and downs, and I don't want to only feel happy during the summers of my life. I desired to have the capacity to find joy in the wintery seasons of trials that would inevitably come my way.

In my search for answers to how to create a happier, more loving, and more consistently incredible life. I finally found the answer. It was in a moment when I was at an event listening to Brandon talk about what state of mind is and how our state of mind affects how we perceive and experience life.

He described the ups and downs of emotions that inevitably happen if we do not manage our state of mind. A fire lit within me, and I became willing to do whatever it took to become the person I wanted to be for myself, my Creator, and my family.

The Battle Within

Have you ever wondered why sometimes you feel like you can do anything while other times, you feel like life is terrible and most definitely not going to work out?

There is nothing wrong with you…we've all been there! What no one tells us is, there is actually a battle going on within us every single day. When Brandon explained this battle and helped me to learn how I could win the battle, my eyes were opened to what was really going on, and I felt empowered to create the life I wanted.

You might be thinking, *what is this battle?* It is a battle between the lion and the hyena. You see, we all have a part of ourselves that is like a lion: empowered, strong, courageous. We also have parts of ourselves that are like a hyena: scared, stuck in scarcity, and angry. We empower the part of ourselves that we feed the most. If we think about and act upon the courageous, strong part of ourselves, our capacity and character grow. If we give space to negative feelings and thoughts and we entertain and act on them, we empower our hyena and get stuck in contention and scarcity.

Once we understand that this battle is going on, we are empowered to take the necessary steps to win the battle within. Part of winning the battle within is learning to quiet our hyena and empower our lion.

This is critical so the lion can be in the driver's seat and guide us in the most important decisions in our life. We win by doing all we can to stay in an empowered state of mind. We need to understand that as we make decisions and act in ways that support our best self, that part of us grows. We also need to understand that we don't need to be ashamed of our hyena because its purpose is to empower our lion. The hyena is trying to protect us, to keep us stuck in a comfortable place.

It's risky to step toward our potential, and it takes a tremendous amount of courage. When we are faced with the real decision of listening to the hyena and staying in a safe, comfortable, stagnant place or taking steps toward our potential and contending with all of uncertainty and faith that requires, we are left with a real choice. We strengthen when we step toward our potential even when it's hard. Without opposition from our hyena, we would not have a real choice.

Pillars of State

The biggest line of defense that helps us to win the battle within is the Pillars of State. This is what holds everything up and allows us to be able to choose who we want to be, even when dealing with crazy circumstances. The reality is that we do not go through life easily.

There are challenges that we all need to face. These challenges strengthen us and help us to become who we need to be, so we can do what we are destined to do.

It is easy to have perspective looking back through the lens of time, but in the thick of it, when the kids are screaming, you aren't sure if you can pay your mortgage this month, the car breaks down again, and your partner uses fighting words, it is not so easy to respond as your best self. It is okay; you are human, and you will feel frustrated, angry, and sad sometimes.

To be in a good state of mind does not mean that you don't give yourself permission to feel those things. It does mean that you can slow down enough to give yourself a little breathing room to respond rather than instantly reacting in a way that you won't feel good about.

When we react to a situation from a place of stress, the part of our brain responsible for dealing with fight or flight is in the driver's seat and often is driving us to a yelling, angry, "it's their fault" town.

When we can give ourselves just a little space between when a situation happens and when we respond, the part of our brain capable of making rational decisions is in the driver's seat instead, and that is what allows us to deal with the situation more calmly. But how do we create enough space to respond in a way which makes us feel good?

The Pillars of State is the tool that allows us the time and perspective we need to respond in the way we want to. Let's dive into the Pillars of State right now.

Pillars of State

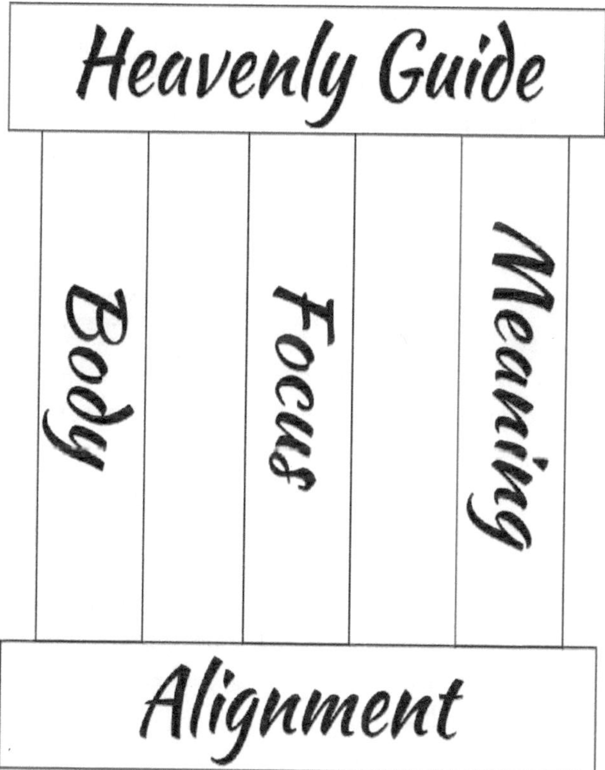

The First Pillar of State – Body

The first Pillar of State is Body. This is because when we move our body, we change our physical environment, and in doing so, we change our state of mind. We can move our body by doing many things; it could be something like jumping jacks, deep breathing, drinking a healthy protein shake, or going for a walk. When we get up and move, endorphins flow through our body, and that helps us to feel better. The reason exercise works so well is because it is a fast way to change your state of mind.

There was a time when I was getting frustrated and reacting to my daughter. I didn't want to feel that way toward my daughter, but when she would throw a temper tantrum, I found myself throwing an emotional temper tantrum right next to her.

I decided I would stop this pattern by doing pushups every time I thought something negative about her. I didn't tell her why I was doing the pushups; I just did them. I figured that I would think more positively about my daughter, or I would get super strong.

Either way, it would be a win! After doing a couple of rounds of pushups, I found it was much easier to notice what my daughter was doing right and commit to being more loving toward her.

I broke the pattern in my mind, so I could create the relationship I want with my daughter.

The Second Pillar of State - Focus

The Second Pillar of State is Focus. What we focus on is what we notice. It becomes how we see the world.

Have you ever been thinking about buying a new car and then suddenly you see the model of the car you are thinking about everywhere? Of course, there wasn't a mad rush for everyone in your community to buy the same car; you're merely noticing them more because you are focused on them.

The same is true when it comes to what we focus on in our relationships with others and with ourselves. If you notice all the things your partner does that annoys you, you will find more things to be annoyed by. If, however, you focus on what you love about your partner, you will begin to see all their incredible qualities.

This happened to me when I decided that I was going to change how I saw my husband. Instead of noticing what he was doing that was driving me crazy, I started a gratitude journal about everything I loved about him.

To be completely honest, at first, I couldn't think of anything. Then I kept asking myself, *what are you grateful for about Andy?* Soon, I started noticing the things he did that I was grateful for. Shortly after, I noticed a lot of things. Then I started telling him what I was grateful for, and he started doing even more things for me to be grateful for!

How is it that we can change our focus in such a powerful way? To answer that question, we need to understand the truth of our minds. It is a little-known fact that our brains are question answering machines.

Meaning, whenever we ask ourselves a question, we are going to get an answer. Ask, *why am I so awesome?* And we are going to receive a lot of reasons why we are great. Ask, *why does life always suck?* And we are going to see a list of reasons why life is terrible. Our brains will always answer the questions that we put in front of them. This is why we need to know how to ask questions that empower our best self.

The wonderful fact about knowing the questions we ask ourselves determines the quality of our life is that we can choose to ask questions that build us up, strengthen us, and help us go in the direction that we want to go.

There are a few questions that will make or break your day and how you experience your life. One question, in particular, is the most powerful question you will ever ask. It is one that can take you from the depths of feeling overwhelmed, lost, confused, guilty, or frustrated to a place of gratitude and learning. It will empower your best self, and it will help you to constantly learn the lessons the Creator is trying to teach you because I promise there is always something the Creator is trying to teach you.

The powerful question that I am talking about is this: "What is the Creator trying to teach me?" As you ask that question, you will receive an answer, and you will begin to see the lessons you need to learn.

Your life will shift from one that is happening to you to one where you are the heroine of your own story. You will be empowered in any situation no matter how challenging, and you will be thrust into an attitude of growth and teachability. You will become a partner with the Creator to learn all that you are destined to learn.

The Third Pillar of State - Meaning

The Third Pillar of State is Meaning. When a circumstance happens, it is not good or bad. We decide if it is good or bad by the meaning we attach to it. Meaning is how we understand our experiences and how we see the world. It is how we understand the world.

I believe that meaning is how two people can go through a similar situation and have a completely different experience. We need to understand that we can change our state of mind by changing the meaning we give to the events that happen in our lives. Let me give you an example.

Let's say, my husband, Andy, comes home late from work…again. I am so angry because I think he didn't bother to check what time it was because he was so busy talking to his buddy at work. When he comes home, I already have a story in my mind about why he is late, and I decided that him being late means that he doesn't care about me. When he walks through the door, am I going to greet him with open arms or contention and anger?

What if when he was late coming home, I just notice that he is late, and I don't come to any conclusions about what that means. Instead, I decided that I am going to talk to him about it when he gets home. When he does get home, I let him know that I know he loves me, and I am sure something important must have come up, but I feel hurt when he isn't home on time.

Then he lets me know that he is sorry for coming home late, but his co-worker had a flat tire that he needed to help fix. How understanding and forgiving do you think I will be once I know the real story? You see, the previous story about him chatting with his buddy was all made up in my mind, and it was simply not true. Hearing and understanding the real story brings us closer together rather than further apart.

As Dr. Kathy Gruver, Ph.D., Stress and Communication Expert, says, "Our body can't distinguish between what we are imagining and what is happening external to ourselves." We need to understand this phenomenon because when we create meaning that is not true, it creates stress.

Our body will physically respond as though it really happened. We need to understand that the meaning we attach to our experiences in life will change how we see our life. That is why affirmations work so powerfully. They help us to see things in a different way. Instead of repeating in our minds, *I am such a bad mom*, we can say, *I am a loving, present, and calm mom.*

When we use our language to change the meaning of our circumstances, we can move away from the meaning that is hurting us, to the meaning that is helping us become who we were meant to be. As Dr. Kathy Gruver says, "By changing our mind to a more positive state, we can change our bodies for the better. We can program our bodies to be healthy, recover quicker, and even stave off illness."

Science backs me up. As Dr. Gruver says in her book *Conquer Your Stress with Mind/Body Techniques*:[4] "In a study by Xu 51, the effect of mind power was tested on the HIV-1 virus. The HIV virus was extracted and placed on a plate; researchers were trained to use visualization in an attempt to influence the structure of the virus. One group concentrated on 'inhibit growth,' one 'increase growth,' and the other was the control.

At the end of the experiment, the HIV that had been infused with the thoughts 'increase' had increased more than the placebo, and in the same vein, the 'inhibit' dish showed less HIV than the control. The results of this study point out that the human mind has the power to influence HIV growth and infectivity."

That study is a powerful example of how much our thoughts impact our bodies and our reality. The really cool thing is that one of the most powerful ways to shift meaning is to switch-up our focus through questions. Start asking yourself what you are grateful for every day, and you will begin to experience a world full of things to be grateful for.

The Fourth Pillar: The Foundation of State - Alignment

Remember when I was talking about alignment earlier? Alignment is critical to the state of mind.

In fact, it is the Foundation of State of Mind. This is because when we are in alignment with the Fire Principles, we get help from the Creator. We are lifted and strengthened by the Divine.

Alignment is the foundation that the rest of the Pillars of State rest upon. Alignment means living a principle-centered life by following the Four Primary Laws of Fire. Without alignment, the other Pillars of State will fall. When we lean on a power greater than ourselves, we stand upon a firm foundation that will strengthen us through the storms of this life.

It is the defining difference between someone who is just positive and hyped up (which doesn't last through the hard times of life, incidentally) and someone who has optimism and peace grounded in a foundation of faith and principles.

The Fifth Pillar: The Capstone of State – The Heavenly Guide

I introduced you to The Heavenly Guide earlier. The Heavenly Guide is the component that most people in the personal development world are missing.

The Heavenly Guide takes state management to the next level as it is the capstone of the state of mind.

It is what helps people go from living an everyday life to living an extraordinary life. It is the guiding force that will comfort you when you are going through difficult circumstances, will help you know truth from deception, and will guide you t through creating and living your purpose. The Heavenly Guide is what will allow you to sanctify your life and become a blessing and inspiration to the people around you.

If you make it a priority to listen to and follow the inspiration of The Heavenly Guide in your life, you will experience magic and adventure that is beyond even the best tales told in the movies.

The fifth pillar of state is the heavenly guide. It is the Divine guidance you receive that will lead you to your purpose and help you create the life you were meant to live. We get access to The Heavenly Guide when the other Pillars of State are in place. When the other Pillars of State are not in place, we cannot access The Heavenly Guide because we can't hear it. When we are too distracted with the circumstances of life and wrapped up in a negative state of mind, we cannot hear the quiet inspirations of The Heavenly Guide.

Morning Empowerment

Now that you know about the Four Primary Laws of Fire, you are ready to create a life that is better than you could have dreamed of.

Sometimes, it is challenging to put the Four Primary Laws of Fire into action in an easy, doable way when you are juggling so many other things.

Don't worry; I have your back! This is an exercise I use that helps me put the Four Primary Laws of Fire into action every single day. It helps me to be less stressed and more present with the people I love.

Brandon and I came up with a series of questions that help direct the mind and empower our greatest selves. These questions are meant to be asked at the beginning of the day if possible because they direct our focus, help us to receive

Divine inspiration, prevent us from being swallowed up in the minutia of life, and in doing so, keep us focused on what matters most.

They are put together in an exercise called the Morning Empowerment. If you do this exercise every day consistently, you will:

- Feel more positive
- Be more balanced throughout your day
- Feel more connected to the Creator
- Feel more loving and connected to the people around you
- Feel happier

That is a big promise, I know, but it is absolutely true.

With exactness means that if you forget to do it for a day, don't worry about it, slips happen. If they do, don't beat yourself up over it; just start your count back at one.

For example, if you do this exercise for 30 days and then miss a day, you'll start back at day one the next day. No guilt, no worries, just an openness to creating a ritual that will give you incredible results in your life. After all, as Zig Ziglar says, "Repetition is the mother of learning and the father of action, which makes it the architect of accomplishment."

Ask yourself the following questions. It is better to write your answers down, but you don't have to.

Digging Deep
Morning Empowerment Exercise

1. What three things am I grateful for?
2. What are two things I can accomplish before 10 am?
3. What are two things the Creator has done for me that I should be grateful for?
4. What are two things someone has done for me that I can be grateful for?
5. How can I brighten my partner or loved one's day?
6. Who can I serve today, and how?
7. What is one thing the Creator wants me to do today?
8. In what ways am I shrinking or holding back in life?
9. What's one thing I could do to step forward to improve?
10. What is something I appreciate about someone else? (Tell them!)

CHAPTER 4:
PRIMARY LAW OF FIRE - ALIGNMENT

"Learn to speak the Lord's language." ~Sheri Dew

ALIGNMENT TO FIRE PRINCIPLES means following the Fire Principles that you know about and being willing to follow the inspiration you get from the Creator.

Doing what the Creator inspires you to do is how you show love to the Creator. It really is an incredible cycle that when we follow the Fire Principles and the inspiration we get from the Creator; we get more inspiration and more blessings. Life becomes an adventure, and we begin to experience miracles firsthand.

I know this might sound a little flaky. If you recall my story, I didn't believe in the Creator when I first started out on this journey, and I most certainly thought I had not seen any miracles. But after aligning to the Fire Principles myself, I can say without a doubt that Fire Principles are true principles. Just stay with me here and be willing to doubt your doubts.

After all, if you want something different in your life, you need to act in a different way.

Sometimes that means taking a leap of faith even when you don't have all the answers. This is not easy, believe me, I know, but it is always worth it.

I can't tell you how many times being in alignment and following inspiration has helped me have incredible conversations with people I have just met and has even saved my life and the lives of my children…several times.

The great thing is that the more we are in alignment with Fire Principles, the easier it is to be in alignment with them. We are in alignment when we know and follow Fire Principles, and we receive and follow inspiration from the Creator.

The blessing we receive from following the Fire Principles is far greater than the energy and sacrifice it took to follow the law. The challenge, though, is that often it is difficult to align to the Fire Principles when we have not yet experienced the blessing from it. We have to do what the Creator wants us to do without tangible evidence that our life will be better because of it. It takes faith and stepping outside our comfort zone. We only get evidence that we are blessed after we align with the Fire Principles. I have experienced this many times in my life.

I remember vividly the day I learned about tithing. Tithing is basically giving away 10 percent of your income to charity. Some people give it to a church, some to charity. At the time, we were over $1200 in the hole every month. There was no extra 10 percent in our budget! I had tried aligning to other Fire Principles, so I knew they were true, but this one I did not want to align to.

I remember talking to my mentor about it and saying, "I just don't have the money to give."
He looked at me and casually said something that would forever change how I felt about tithing.

He said, " the Creator does not need your money. The Creatorneeds you to learn how to give." That one statement cut to my core andhelped me face one of my deepest, darkest secrets.

I believe in giving, and I spent many years serving people in need. I even walked the early morning streets of Edmonton, Alberta, helping homeless people for years. I always wanted to give more, but I never felt like I could. Giving 10 percent felt like something I just couldn't do. I knew I needed to do it, though. It was a feeling within me.

I will never forget the day I wrote the check to give to charity. I sealed the envelope and then walked to the mailbox and stood outside, staring at it for several minutes. I reached out and pulled down the mailbox handle. It was one of those old-fashioned types that stand on the street corner. The handle might as well have weighed a ton with how much effort it took me to open it.

Then eyes closed, I dropped the envelope into the mail and quickly let the handle close before I could change my mind. Once the deed was done, I walked away with relief and fear. I didn't know how it was going to work out for us. We didn't have the money to pay for it, but I did it anyway. We took action in aligning to the principle before we knew how it would work out.

Do you know what happened? One day, we were struck with an idea that turned our financial situation around. We got an inspiration that made us realize that we were sitting on the answer to our problems the whole time.

An opportunity to host overseas exchange students in our home came up. Having two students in our home would mean that we would get to help out and get to know kids from around the world, and our income would make an extra $1400 a month. This turned our financial situation around and gave us some breathing room in our budget!

I tell you this story because I want you to see how alignment works. Notice that we didn't get the inspiration to turn our finances around until we gave money away for tithing. Notice that the answer to our problems did not come with a magical check in the mail. Rather, the answer came from us pondering possible solutions, finding more information and them, and taking action. The answers that we get to resolve our individual challenges will be different for everyone, but I promise you that there are answers waiting for you. You just need to learn how to ask for and how to hear the answer.

Meet Your Heavenly Guide

Most of my life, I didn't know that there is a Creator, there are Fire Principles, and that there is a way to talk directly to and receive messages from the Creator.

As a teenager, I lost my dad to cancer and spent many years being angry at the Creator. I wanted to live my purpose in life and to feel like I was living an inspired life, but a part of me knew that I couldn't do it on my own.

I will never forget the day that Brandon told me that I could receive direct inspiration from the Creator to live my purpose. I wanted to believe it, but I was scared. What if it wasn't real? What if what he suggested didn't work for me? What if he was crazy? Luckily none of these things were true. I decided that I would take a leap of faith and doubt my doubts.

I remember walking through the woods in a pine forest in Canada in the winter with the ground covered with puffy, white snow. I was alone in the woods, and there was a feeling of stillness and serenity. I started just talking to the Creator in my mind and asking if the Creator was real.

At first, I didn't get answers, and I worried that I wouldn't get any. Then in a moment that changed everything, I received an undeniable answer from the Creator. Using the Three Keys to Receiving Inspiration (which I will share with you in the coming pages), I knew that the Creator was, in fact, real and that I could communicate directly with Him.

For me, that was game-changing because I finally felt like a part of me was filled. I wasn't alone anymore, and I began to get a sense that there was something big for me to do. Now that I knew how to communicate with the Creator, I can't begin to tell what an incredible blessing that has been for me. It has allowed me to know that Fire Principles are true, helped me to get direction in my life when I feel stuck, and helped me to feel peace when life gets hard. It has even saved my life and the lives of my children and husband.

Let me tell you a story about when this has saved my family's lives. I was driving along a winding road with my family on the way back from a camping trip. The road was narrow and was on the top of a cliff. We were having a good time listening to music and talking about the great time we had camping.

When all of a sudden, my husband Andy received Divine guidance that he should swerve the car wheel toward the cliff. My heart jumped as I watched our car suddenly go toward the edge of the cliff, and I screamed! At that very moment, a big red truck came speeding around the corner in our lane. Because of Andy's direct guidance from the Heavenly Guide to swerve the car, we just missed hitting the truck, and he quickly turned the wheel back toward the road and away from the cliff. Once I caught my breath again, I realized that if he had not turned the car toward the cliff, we would have hit the truck head-on, and likely; our car would have been thrown off the side of the cliff due to the impact of the collision. Andy's quick response and Divine guidance saved our lives!

After taking a few moments to recover, I asked Andy how he knew to swerve the wheel before he saw the truck. He said he had a feeling that he needed to swerve the car, and he followed that inspiration from the Heavenly Guide without knowing there was a truck about to come around the corner in our lane.

The feeling he got that guided him to make that decision came from something that I call the Heavenly Guide. That voice from the Creator saved our lives that day. I am so grateful for the knowledge of the Heavenly Guide, and I am grateful that my husband was acting in a way that he could hear that still small prompting.

I know that everyone in the world has this gift within them, too, and just needs a little help to find it. You have it, and once you know how to talk to the Creator, you will be set free in a way you cannot possibly imagine. I know there are big things for you to do. Things that only you have the talent and ability to accomplish. You will be able to do all that the Creator desires for you when you know how to be a team with the Creator.

Knowledge about how to communicate with the creator did not come from me. I learned about it from spiritual leaders and a pure source of truth.

For you to be a team with the Creator, you need to understand a few things about how communication with the Creator works.

The first thing you need to know is that communicating with the Creator is two-way communication. You can talk to the Creator, but you need to be able to listen to His answers. The way the Creator speaks to you is in a calm, quiet way. We need to understand that because if we are stuck in feelings like anger, frustration, fear, or other consuming emotions, we will not be able to hear the voice of the Creator.

The second thing we need to understand is that the Creator speaks to us through something Brandon calls the Heavenly Guide. Some people call the Heavenly Guide by different names such as spirit, inner light, or intuition, or the Light of Christ. In the context of this book, I will call it the Heavenly Guide.

The Heavenly Guide is a spirit that lives outside of us and is a gift given to everyone that allows us to receive communication from the Creator.

The third thing we need to know is that the Heavenly Guide usually communicates with us through thoughts and feelings. We can ask the Heavenly Guide questions, and we will get answers by paying attention to how we feel.

It is best to ask the Heavenly Guide yes or no questions so we can receive a clear answer. To get a yes answer from the Heavenly guide, we often experience a peaceful feeling in our stomach or burning in our chest. If we get an answer of no from the Heavenly guide, we will feel tension, or a crunchy feeling in our stomach or chest. If we don't get an answer, it means that we need to make a decision before we can get an answer. This is because the Creator did not create us to be followers. He Created us to make decisions and become the people He knows we can be, and often, that involves deciding for ourselves.

The fourth thing we need to understand is that the Heavenly Guide will only give us answers that bring us closer to the Creator and closer to our potential. That means we will only receive answers that bring more good into our life. Sometimes we are given hard truths and may not like the answers we get, but we will never receive an answer that would bring harm to ourselves or someone else.

The fifth thing we need to understand is what the Heavenly Guide can do. The Heavenly Guide can confirm the truth, give us answers to spiritual questions, confirm the truth of the existence of the Creator, warn us of danger, and give us comfort.

Now that you understand how communicating with the Creator works, you are ready to get your own answers and inspiration. These are the Three Keys to Receiving Inspiration that has helped me so much. I am so excited to share them with you.

1. Ask with a desire to know.
2. Listen for the answer.
3. Act on the inspiration you receive.

I promise you that the Heavenly Guide is real and that it is there to help you get through the chaos of this life. In the context of this book, I cannot go much deeper in explaining the Heavenly Guide; however, if you desire more information about spiritual principles, contact me, and I will get you in touch with someone who can go into deeper spiritual principles than I can in this book.

Digging Deep

Now that you know about the Heavenly Guide, are you willing to put your trust to the test and begin a relationship with the Heavenly Guide that will change your life forever?

The only thing left for you to do is ask your question. I promise that if you do this with pure intent, you will get the answers you desire, and you will begin this incredible journey of talking directly with your Creator.

You will be empowered to live up to who you are meant to be.

CHAPTER 5:
PRIMARY LAW OF FIRE - SERVICE

"I alone cannot change the world, but I can cast a stone across the waters to create many ripples." ~Mother Teresa

THIS PRIMARY LAW OF FIRE relates to making more money, feeling joy, and living your true purpose.

To understand how service relates to receiving all of these great things in life, let me begin by sharing with you one of the biggest mistakes that women entrepreneurs make that causes them not to receive the money or happiness they are looking for.

The pendulum of service is simple. On one side of the pendulum is what we want to create. Let's say we want to make more money. On the other side of the pendulum is something that most people completely leave out, so they don't get the results they want. In fact, what most people do is chase after the money, trying to get more money.

Meaning, most people chase after money in a state of desperation and, in doing so, repel any potential customers or opportunities. We do this when we take the job; we don't really want or start a business; we don't really care about to get more money.

This also happens when we go after a customer with the sole purpose of making more money. The problem or issue with this approach is that people feel it, and it repels them. The boss feels that you are just in it for the money, so you don't get the promotion, and you are the first one to be let go when the company makes cutbacks. The customer feels your desperation and that you are just looking for a sale and so they don't buy. The business partner goes behind your back and makes side deals that end up cutting your profits because the culture of your business is that everyone is just in it for the money. With this attitude, no one wins, and usually, either no one makes money, or the money that is made is quickly lost.

So, what is the alternative? To understand this, we need to understand that on the other side of the pendulum, the thing that creates the financial results we want is something that is often talked about and rarely understood.

The thing we actually need to go after is service. I know what you're thinking, *yeah, like I need to serve more!* I thought that too. In fact, I remember the first time that Brandon shared this principle with me and how I was thinking, *you have got to be kidding me! I serve in my family, in my community, and I feel like I have nothing more to give, and now you are telling me I need to serve to make more money?* If my facial expressions could have screamed, they would have.

If you remember, at the time I first met Brandon, I was in debt over $100,000. I was desperate to make more money. I was also feeling completely burnt out and overwhelmed. Andy and I had started our own business and were working until nearly midnight every day in our business and juggling our day jobs.

I wanted to be able to breathe easier at night and not be a workaholic, and that required our bank balance to go up. I remember trying to make sales calls in our business and being so hungry for the sale that I was just focused on that. The call felt weird, and at the end of it, the person did not buy. I felt completely defeated. I needed to learn a way to move people to a yes, but how?

When Brandon explained that we need to serve with real intent to have more money, I realized that is what I was missing. At the time, I had partnered with a company that I didn't care about, and I didn't think I was really serving people through my work. I was compromising on my values, and it came at a cost.

I re-evaluated everything I was doing, and Andy and I started a new business that helped people in their relationships. It was a relationship retreat in the middle of the mountains, and I loved it. When I talked to people about the retreat, I was fired up! I desperately wanted to help them improve their marriages, and I knew they could do it by applying the principles we were teaching, the principles that Brandon taught us.

Although we no longer run this business, I will never forget a lesson I learned one weekend in a cozy cabin in the mountains that helped me understand how the Principle of Service is critical to my business.

There was one night when I was about to move in for the close and invite people to buy a ticket to an event we were running that would help them even more, But I froze. I was about to offer them an opportunity to keep working with us when suddenly, I was terrified to ask for the sale.

My friends were in that room, and I didn't want anyone to feel sold or feel weird. Then in a moment, I was transformed.

It was like I put on a superhero cape and was willing to push through my discomfort and uncertainty and fear to help the people in that room. I realized that I wanted to help them create the results in their lives more than I cared about how afraid I was about how they would perceive me.

I stepped in front of that room and boldly declared, "I hate selling, but I know that what we are offering will help you transform your relationships, and I want you to have everything you deserve, so I am going to do it anyway. Can I tell you about the event that's coming up?"

Right then and there, I saw that service can be and should be at the heart of all business. It is what everything else is based upon and is the very thing that keeps us pushing forward when things get tough, and when we feel tired, and we are worried about how others will think about us. It is the thing that will allow us to do great things in this life, and that will help us achieve the financial success that we desire.

Obligation vs. Service

When I first learned about the importance of serving others, I felt overwhelmed because I didn't fully understand what service means. I have been conditioned to help others. It has always been expected of me, and I expected it of myself, but sometimes service felt exhausting, and I was left feeling like I had nothing more to give.

I remember the first time I expressed this to Brandon, and he asked me a couple of questions that helped me to understand what service is and what it is not.

This small distinction has helped me to be uplifted and strengthened by service rather than feeling tired and burnt out. It has been a game-changer and something I think that every woman needs to know.

I was struggling with the idea that to create the life I wanted with more money, more happiness, and more connection to the people I love; I would need to serve more. I was already feeling stretched, and my to-do list seemed endless and a little terrifying.

I wanted things to be different, but how could I possibly do more? I approached Brandon after the event and asked him how I could possibly be expected to serve more when I was already stretched so thin. He looked at me intently and then asked me a question that changed everything and helped me understand what service is and how it would help me light the fire within me again.

The question he asked was, "How do you feel after you serve

someone?"

I said, "Well, usually, I am tired and stressed out, and sometimes I feel a little resentful."

He went on to explain that there is a difference between serving out of obligation and out of true love for the other person. I thought about that for a moment. He then went on to say, "You can tell if you are serving out of obligation or serving out of love by how you feel. When you serve someone out of obligation, you will feel low energy, but when you serve someone out of love, you will feel more energy."

I reflected on this for a moment and thought back to times in my life when I had served someone out of obligation. I remember one time helping one of my relatives who was always asking for favors and who wasn't very kind to me because of some mental health challenges she was going through.

I helped her, but, to be completely frank, I didn't want to. I resented her for it, and I felt drained afterward. Once I understood the difference between true service and obligation, I resolved that I would focus on serving people out of love and that I would stop allowing myself to be dragged down by obligation.

The first time I was given an opportunity to practice this new resolve didn't go as smoothly as I had hoped. I was again asked to help this relative. I said yes, and feelings of resentment began to creep in. I decided that I would act differently this time and focus on loving her no matter what.

I resolved that no matter what she did or said, I would be loving and that I would set limits and only help her when I really could help her instead of dropping everything the moment she asked for help. It was incredible how much differently I saw the situation after this. I actually felt more loving toward her and wasn't affected as much when she was unkind. I had more energy after helping her and was more willing to help her the next time.

It is not always easy to serve this way, out of love, and with real intent, but it is definitely worth it! I have found that I love serving, and when I do it with the right intent, I have more energy, feel more loving to the people around me, and closer to my Creator.

After all, as my biggest mentor and teacher, Jesus Christ says, "For whosoever will save his life shall lose it: and whosoever will lose his life for my sake shall find it." Matthew 16:25.

I love how Mahatma Gandhi explains, "The best way to find yourself is to lose yourself in the service of others."

From this, we can learn that the best way to find ourselves is to serve others. It is in the process of helping others that we are transformed and become more of who we were always meant to be.

Accepting Help

We have talked about the importance of giving service to others, but what is rarely talked about is the importance of being willing to receive help. We try to be independent, confident, and strong women who have it all together.

The reality, though, is that we all have weaknesses, and we all have struggles that we have to go through. We need each other. It is often so easy to reach out to someone else when you see they need help, but it can be the most difficult thing in the world to ask for help when we are the ones in need.

Let's be honest here; it hurts our pride. I struggle with this one. I don't want to feel weak; I don't want to feel like I can't do it on my own, I don't want to rely on others when life throws me a crazy curveball. Sometimes though, we need to be willing to put our pride aside and openly, with grateful hearts accept support from others.

After I had my third baby, I remember being in survival mode. I wasn't sleeping much during the night for weeks on end. I was going through my days in a haze of sleeplessness and numbness. The most basic tasks of doing laundry and having a shower seemed insurmountable. I had recently moved to a new country where I didn't know many people, and I felt alone.

I tried desperately to keep up with household chores, but really, it was a miracle if the toys were picked up at the end of the day.

Let's just say vacuuming and cleaning bathrooms hadn't made the done list, and my house felt a little on gross.
I was wearing my yoga pants (the same ones I had been wearing for three days), and I had baby spit up all over my shoulder. I heard a buzzing sound from my phone, and I looked down to see a text that told me that someone I barely knew was bringing over dinner.

A feeling of relief and panic flooded over me simultaneously. I was relieved at the idea of not having to make dinner. Not only did I not know what I was going to make, but I was also pretty sure I didn't have any ingredients to make said mystery dinner. I felt panic at the idea of someone coming into my home the way it was to witness the mess and chaos that I found myself in.

I responded to the text: "Oh, that's okay... I am doing fine. Thanks anyway."

They texted back, "Really, I want to bring dinner over for your family if you can use it."

I could've really used it, but I didn't want to burden anyone, and I certainly didn't want them to have to walk into our messy and dirty house!

It was then that I realized that my pride was stopping me from receiving help and love from others. At that moment, I understood that the Creator cared about me and saw how overwhelmed I was feeling and was sending someone to help me. I was allowing my pride to get in the way of the help He was sending.

I took a deep breath, swallowed my pride, and texted back, "That would be incredible. Thank you so much!"

My neighbor arrived with the meal, came into my house, and gave me a hug. I am so grateful for the lesson I learned that day. It was not easy for me to accept help, but when I began to understand that the Creator uses all of us to help each other, I could feel the Creator's love for me.

Being willing to accept help has been so incredible. Now I have been able to create support systems with other moms supporting each other with trading babysitting and helping each other when we are sick or when life gets crazy. Life is too crazy to do it on our own. We need other people, and they need us.

Digging Deep

What is one thing you can do to focus on service more (in your business, your community, your family, and your relationships)?

How can you be even more open to receiving service from others?

CHAPTER 6:
PRIMARY LAW OF FIRE - GROWTH

"I know God will not give me anything I can't handle. I just wish that He didn't trust me so much." ~Mother Teresa

HAVE YOU EVER FELT stuck in your life, like you are going through the motions but not feeling the joy you want?

We can often get so caught up in the minutia of life that we stop dreaming and stop working toward our goals. Our to-do lists can become our master, and we are left running from one thing to the next.

So in between all of the things we have to do, how can we feel like we are moving forward rather than being lost in the chaos of life? The answer, of course, is that we need to be growing constantly. Growing is the constant act of moving forward toward our greatest potential.

As Steven Covey said, "To know and not to do is really not to know."

It is in the application of knowledge that we build our strength of character, overcome challenges, and gain the confidence we need to learn more.

Just think about a runner. Is a person a runner if they know how to run and think about running? Do their leg muscles get stronger by doing that? I wish! But they need to get out there, move their butts, and actually run.

The same is true with growth. Once we learn something, we need to get out there and try it. Often when we are just learning something and taking action on new information, it can feel awkward and forced as if we aren't good at it, so *why bother?*

That is one of the biggest tricks of the hyena because it is so natural for things to feel weird when we are trying something new. Think about a baby learning to walk. Does the baby just jump right up and start running, or is she wobbly, falling down often, getting back up and trying again? Every time that baby gets back up, she gets stronger and knows more about how to do what she is trying to do.

The same is true with us as we are practicing new skills and learning new things. It feels weird at first; we feel wobbly in our skills, we fall down, we get back up and try again. It is the very act of getting back up that makes us stronger and closer to succeeding. So be patient with yourself, trust the process, and go for it!

Angela Duckworth helps us understand how important it is to have a growth mindset so that we have the determination required to achieve our goals when she said that "Talent counts, effort counts twice." This helps us understand that we do not need natural talent to succeed.

In fact, having the willingness to take determined, consistent effort is a better determinant of our success.

Failure is Learning

I know that many people in the personal development industry say that we need to be okay with failure and that it is part of the process.

However, in the trenches, when we really mess up, being ok with failure is easier said than done. It is easy to beat up on ourselves and replay the event in our minds trying to understand how we could have possibly messed up so badly. And although it makes absolutely no sense to do this instant replay of mistakes, we often do it, and it changes nothing.

Well, actually, it changes everything. It changes our perspective and keeps us focused on the past and thinking negatively about ourselves instead of taking the lesson and being propelled into the future where we can actually change things.

There was a point in my journey of shifting from my 9-5 job to starting our business when I made a bad business decision. At the time, my husband and I were desperate for a solution to our financial problems of being nearly $100,000 in debt and $1200 in the hole each month.

We were naive and did not know how to sift through the empty promises of the personal development world. We joined one company that promised us an exceptional return on investment, and it seemed pretty easy. We just needed to give an investor our cash, and they would give us 10 percent back every month. This investor lent out our money and other investor's money to various companies. The problem was that none of this investment was secured.

So for two months, we happily received $600 from the investment. In the third month, we received a phone call letting us know that the investor had gone bankrupt, and our $60,000 was gone.

At first, I was devastated. At that point in our life, that was a lot of money!

I forced myself to think of 10 things I was grateful for about losing that money. I know it sounds like a stretch...and it was, but eventually, I realized that if I hadn't lost all that money, I would have kept working with the company that was leading us to bad deals, and we would have lost a whole lot more money.

I learned that it is in the failures that we can be led to success. I also realized that I needed to learn how to make my own money rather than relying on the knowledge of others. I needed to be in control of my life and my finances. I knew it would not be an easy journey, and I was right about that, but I also knew it would be worth it.

Even though we know failure is part of success, it often sucks a little...or a lot! No one wants to feel like we can't do something, and it is tough on the ego to admit that we need help or that we have failed.

However, it is critical for us to understand that failure leads to success and that each small step we take toward our goals is essential to creating the results we want. Otherwise, we will become paralyzed by inaction and fear. We need to let go of the guilt and shame that comes with feeling the need to be perfect. So how do we move past the ideas we hold about failure so we can move past our weaknesses and missteps toward the success we desire?

It begins with learning to be able to win the battle within. Language is critical to winning this battle, and the language we use when we mess up helps color the story of the situation. If we are constantly telling ourselves, *how could I have done that? Why am I so stupid?* Our brains are answering machines and will come up with a million reasons to answer those poor-quality questions, and we will stay stuck in the guilt and regret of our mistake.

Incredibly, research shows that our minds gravitate toward thinking negatively because of something called the negativity bias. Dr. Rick Hanson, a neuroscientist, and author of *Buddha's Brain*, explains: "Negative stimuli produce more neural activity than do equally intensive positive ones. They are also perceived more easily and quickly."[5]

Basically, according to Dr. Hanson, this means that "Good experiences bounce off the brain, but bad experiences sink right in." Research also shows that when we think negatively often, our brain actually changes, and it becomes easier to think negatively in the future.

This tells us that we need to be mindful of our thoughts and that we need to know how to create and focus on the positive so we can learn from our mistakes instead of allowing them to define us. In order for us to push past our errors, we need to see them for what they are, steps to help us learn and grow.

I learned this life-changing lesson from my six-year-old daughter. I made a mistake and said, "Oh shoot, I just messed up, Arya."

She looked up at me with her beautiful blue eyes and said, "That's great, Mommy! That means you're learning!"

I am so grateful for my daughter and the lesson she taught me that day about what failure really means. When we don't have our kids to remind us, we need to remind ourselves that when we mess up, we just need to get back up and learn from the mistake.

What if when you made a mistake, you told yourself, *it's okay to make mistakes, they are teaching me something.* Even better, what if every time you made a mistake, you asked, *what is the lesson?* Would that bring you closer to your ultimate potential? Would that prevent you from making the same mistakes over and over and help you to grow?

The Edge

Any time we want to make a change in this life, we step up to an edge. An edge of our understanding, our knowledge, our comfort level. We stand on the edge of what we believe we can do.

I have faced many of those edges in my life. The edge to get married, the edge of having kids, the edge to start a business, the edge to birth two of my babies at home with no medication, the edge of buying real estate, the edge to move to another country, the list could go on and on.

However, through all of this, I have learned that there a couple of predictable things that happen at the fringe of our comfort zone. If we don't understand the dynamics of the edge, we can easily be swayed to back away from the brink of opportunities that lie in front of us.

It is in these moments that we either move forward toward our divine destiny or stay stuck on the couch of mediocrity. This is a very dangerous position to be in, though, because to experience your purpose and the most incredible parts of this life, we need to step off our edges.

After all, giving up is contagious. We are spiritually and emotionally dying when we back away from opportunities that can stretch us and help us move toward our potential. Let me save you some of the pain that comes from backing away from the edge.

In this next section, I will uncover the dynamics of the edge and how to move forward toward your purpose powerfully.

Dynamic #1: All edges are scary

Have you ever stepped up to the edge of a cliff and looked over it? It is terrifying, right? The steep drop-off reveals lots of sharp pointy rocks that would really hurt if they came in contact with your head.

When we look over the edge, we feel this rush of fear, anxiety, and awe. The same is true at the edges of our understanding. When we are faced with a challenge that stretches our understanding or capacity, that is an edge…and it is uncomfortable and scary.

Dynamic #2: Your lion and hyena will both be roaring

When we approach an edge of our understanding, we need to know that both our lion and our hyena will be invited to the party.

Can you guess which one is going to be the loudest, most obnoxious guest? You got it, the hyena. The hyena will be right by your side, telling you all the reasons you should not step off the edge. "It's too hard," "You don't know how," "You've tried before and failed," anything that will keep you sitting comfortably on the couch of mediocrity.

Luckily for us, though, the lion will also be at the party. Your lion or that part of yourself that is your best self is there pushing you forward, reminding you that your potential is at stake. At that moment, you are faced with a question.

"Which one will I listen to?" The voice you listen to at the edge will be the one that wins.

Dynamic #3: When we back away from the edge

If you listen to the hyena, you will justify your reasons for doing nothing at all and will even call it a "win."

You will cite all the millions of excuses that justify your decision not to take action. You will lose capacity that you otherwise could have built, lose out on the opportunity that was in front of you, and will be more likely to back away from the next edge.

Dynamic #4: Stepping forward at the edge

When you move forward at the edge and take the next step towards the opportunity in front of you in faith, even when you don't know what will happen after that, even if it is death defyingly scary, an incredible thing will happen.

The Creator will meet you on the other side, and another steppingstone will appear. In doing so, your capacity to deal with new edges increases, and you are more likely to take action the next time an opportunity that stretches you appears.

As you look back from the other side of the edge, you will find that you are one step closer to your destiny.

Dynamic #5: *It's not about the edge*

When I first began to understand the dynamics of the edge, I thought it was all about the next step.

That it was about the opportunity lying in front of us. Like starting a new business or doing something that is outside of our comfort zone.

When, in fact, it's not about the next step at all. It is about the faith that is required to take the next step forward when you can't see how it's going to work out. You see, when we are standing at the edge in fear, anxiety, and doubt, and we take a step forward anyway, that requires a tremendous amount of courage and faith.

The Creator meets us, thereby lifting us, strengthening us, and providing the next step. Each step taken in faith builds our connection with the Divine and increases our capacity to live up to who we are meant to be. My mentor helped me to understand that it's not about the next step at all, it's about the level of trust we have in the Creator to be there when we feel like we are going to fall.

The Edge

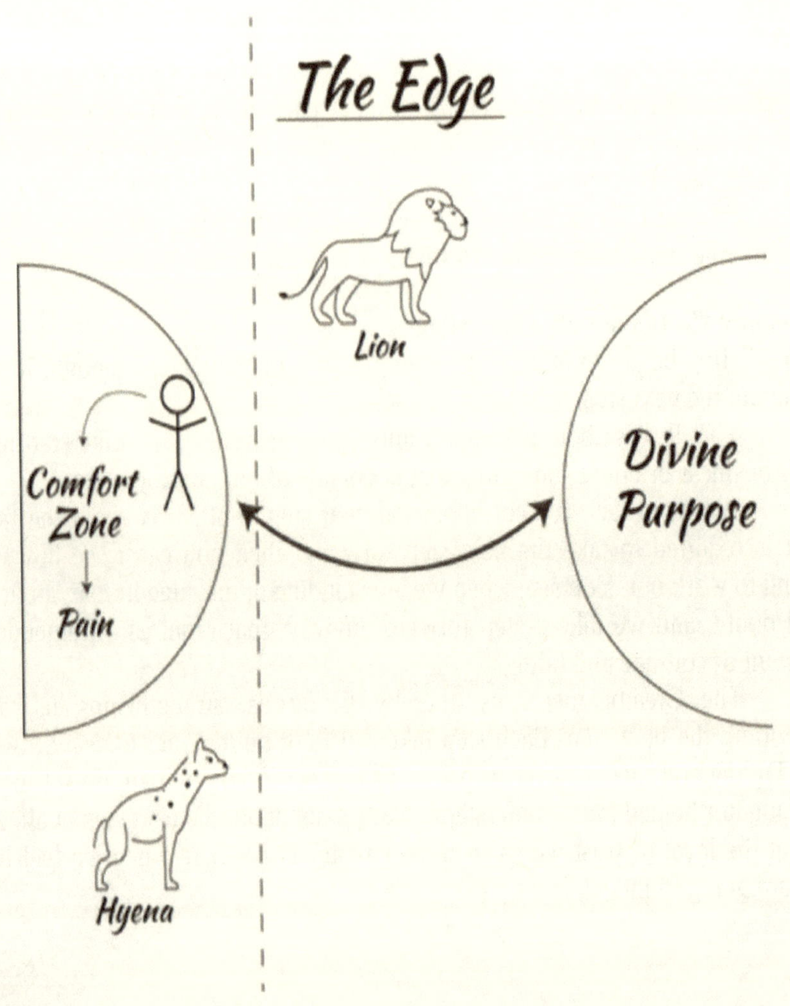

My Big Leap

I was in the smallest airplane I have ever seen in my entire life with duct tape lining the inside of the plane, appearing to hold it together. I was in a gray jumpsuit and had a parachute attached to my back. I was sitting with my legs outstretched with a stranger behind me, whose job it was to make sure we both didn't die. I was terrified. I had always wanted to skydive, but it was right up there on my *holy crap, I don't think I can do it* list. My heart was beating so hard it felt like it would jump out of my chest.

The time came for me to step out onto the wing, and somehow, I took small steps toward the edge of the plane. I remember yelling in my head, *what the heck was I thinking*? But there was no turning back. I was on edge. I took a deep breath and jumped off.

I felt my body plummet through the clouds. My heart was racing, the wind was pounding my face, and I was going so fast that I could hardly see.

Beyond terrified, then a cord was pulled, and suddenly, we were floating through the sky, looking at the breathtaking view below. I was exhilarated, in awe of the beauty around me with the winding river and mountainous landscape.

I realized at that moment that the only way I could have seen that incredible view was to jump out of an airplane. I began to see that if I could face all the edges in my life with courage even when I am scared and keep taking the next step even when I don't know how then the most breathtaking experiences can happen.

That act of jumping out of the airplane for me was life changing. It helped me to understand the dynamics of what happens at the edge of our understanding in a way that nothing else could. I didn't change the world by jumping out of that plane, but that experience changed me.

I saw that I could face one of my biggest fears and overcome them. I learned that in the midst of fear, there is beauty if I can stop, take a deep breath, and look for it. I learned that the Creator is with me and that this world is more beautiful when I can see it from a different perspective. I understood that if I back away from the edges of my comfort zone and understanding, I miss opportunities and a view of what could have been.

I know how important it is to get support when we are approaching our edges. If you would like support from a Fire Within Coach about strategies you can use to overcome the edge that is in front of you, go to www.myfirewithin.com/resources.

Digging Deep

What edge are you facing in your life right now?

We all face edges, whether it's in our business, relationships, or in doing something we are afraid of.

What is that one thing that you know you need to do but are afraid to do it?

How can you see that edge in a new way, so you can take a step forward toward your potential?

CHAPTER 7:
SECRET #2 YOU WITH FIRE

"If you don't like something, change it. If you can't change it, change your attitude." ~Maya Angelou

Change Your Beliefs to Achieve Your Dreams
IN THIS LIFE, we can be told so many things about who we are. We get these messages from all around us; our parents, our friends, the people who don't like us, the people we don't like, and the media, just to name a few.

There is a constant barrage about who everyone else thinks we are and who we "should" be. We try to ignore the criticism of our spouse or the negative comment of another parent from school, but really, they eat away at us just a little bit. As women, we are given so many messages about who we should be. The pressure of all the shoulds "shoulding" all over us is a weight that can drag us down into despair and a feeling of not being good enough.

We are told that we need to be smart but not nerdy smart, sexy, but not sleazy, fun, but not irresponsible. We feel we need to be superwoman… our clothes not only perfectly matching but also clean (if you have little babies you know how hard this one can be), our house spotless,
our lawns perfectly manicured with an organic flower and vegetable garden, and our hair and makeup done when we put the perfect homemade meal on the table. We feel pressured to be the perfect wife, never nagging our husbands. The perfect mother, never being frustrated with our kids and always being the model of love and patience. We are told that we need to have it all figured out…our finances in order, our kids in every activity they can possibly do, be experts at cooking, cleaning, and even sex.

But what if all those expectations that we and others put on us are pure crap? What if they are not only unnecessary but are the very things that would prevent us from being who we truly are and becoming who we are meant to be? What if we don't have to be perfect? What if we just need to be perfectly striving towards improvement and our potential?

Myths of Who We Believe We Are
I recall thinking to myself as a teenager; *I'm so fat!*
And yet as I look back at pictures during that time, I was quite slim.

In fact, I was skinnier than I have ever been to. So why is it that we can rob ourselves of the joy within the now? What if right now at this very moment we are enough? What if the trials, struggles, and experiences we are going through at this junction in time are exactly what we need to learn the lessons we need to learn? What if these lessons and who we are now are what is required to become who we truly are meant to be? What if we are enough...smart enough, pretty enough, skinny enough, brave enough? What if when we accept that we are enough that allows the door of opportunity to open and reveal our potential?

I remember when I was in sixth grade and puberty hit with all the changes in my body and emotions that came along with it. I was awkward and insecure and searching for acceptance outside myself. Small peach fuzz had appeared on my face, and I was mortified.

Unfortunately, a bully in my class also noticed this and picked up this new addition to my upper lip, and he pointed it out...not just to me, of course, but to anyone within earshot. I began to take on the unkind words of the bully, and soon, when I looked into the mirror, all I could see was that one insecurity staring back at me. I couldn't see anything else, and I began to take on the identity of someone who is ugly. I secretly used every technique I could to physically change my appearance in hopes that it would help me to feel beautiful and loved.

Many years later, as an adult, I was talking with a friend of mine who casually talked about having the same issue that I had experienced as a teen. However, there was something different about the way she talked about it. For her, it was just a normal part of growing up, something that a little wax and a little courage could easily take care of.

I looked at her with disbelief that she would talk about what I had previously thought was such a shameful thing. Then the realization hit me that it was not just me that was dealing with that body change, that this was a pretty common issue that many women faced but just didn't talk about. I realized that it didn't define who I am and that I could be beautiful even though I was not perfect and that the haunting teasing of bullies in the past did not have to stay with me.

Why do I tell you that story? I tell you because we all have skeletons in our closet about who we have been told we are. Maybe it is an unkind teacher, a parent who said something mean in anger, a sister or brother who lashed out at us, or a bully at school. Maybe it was a feeling of unworthiness from the barrage of media images about who we are supposed to be.

However, those beliefs about who we are came to be; I want you to know that you no longer need to believe them. That they are not true. That you are so much more. That you have a divine destiny and purpose that is greater than what you can possibly imagine. You get to choose who you are from here on out!

For Things to Change, I Must Change

Today is the beginning of the rest of your life. What do you want to change in your life? Do you want to create more financial success? Do you want to make a difference in the world? Do you want to have incredible relationships? Do you want to be healthier and more fit?

Whatever you want to change in this life, there is one thing that will make all the difference. This one thing is to make or break. It decides your fate and can either empower you to create the changes you want or block you from what you desire most.

What is this one thing I am talking about? I'll give you a hint. You know it well. It is with you at all times. Have you guessed it yet? Once you know what it is, you will be truly empowered to do what it takes to create the life you want. The one thing that makes all the difference is you.

As Jim Rohn says, "For things to change, I must change. For things to be better, I must be better." I know this sounds simple, but it is profound. If you truly want something different in your life, you are going to need to be the one that makes changes within yourself to make it happen.

It is up to you to put in the hard work to create the changes you want. This is true in every context. If you want more money, you are going to need to learn to build a business or invest in real estate to make more money.

You want to be more fit; you are going to need to learn to do the exercises and get complete nutrition through the right food and supplements to create a healthier and more fit you.

So, what has to change within you to create this evolution of becoming who you need to be? First, you need a desire to create the change you want. You have to want it. Then you need to believe that it is possible.

Sometimes this takes seeing someone else do it first, so you can see that it is possible. Then you need to be motivated to do what it takes. Your desire has to be strong enough to push past the times you feel like giving up, the times when you don't know what to do, and the times when your excuses become louder than your desires.

Next, you will require the patience to keep doing what it takes before you see the results you want. It takes time, and although change is happening, sometimes it is hard to see. The last thing you need to create the change you want is a willingness to keep going. What is the point of creating an awesome change in your life only to see all the hard work you did go up in smoke when you stop working at it? I love the quote by Autumn Calabrese that says, "If you want to stop starting over, stop giving up."

If you want to keep the results you fought so hard to get, you need to understand that you are in it for the long haul. Perfection is not required, but perfectly striving is.

The next thing that is critical to understand in creating the results you want in this life is to know that you only have control over yourself.

So often I hear people say that they want to create a change in their lives, but they are waiting for their partner to turn themselves around first, so they can make the change they want. I am here to tell you some good news and some bad news.

The good news is that you absolutely have control over yourself, and you can create incredible changes in your life. The power to do so is already within you, and it is tangible. The bad news is that you cannot change someone else, and the faster you realize this, the better off you will be.

When we spend our time trying to change someone else, we just waste our own energy. When you focus on making the changes you want in yourself, it is incredible how others will respond, and you will inspire them by your example.

In my work coaching many women, I have seen that when they focus on improving themselves rather than trying to change their partner, that they get better results in their relationship and are happier. When they decide to do the right thing no matter what their partner decides to do, there is a confidence and strength that comes out.

Often, they go back into their relationship with a determination to be more loving with themselves and the people around them, and a commitment to live in priority, and you know what happens? When their partner starts seeing them happier and getting the results that they want in their life, their partner eventually asks how they did it because they want results, too!

I have seen this so many times that it is predictable. Work on being the best version of you possible, focus on being the most loving you can be to the people around you, and you will inspire others by your example.

I remember one time when I was so frustrated with my daughter. She was having tantrums, and when she was losing it, I found it hard to keep my cool. One day, when she was having a particularly wild tantrum, I feared that her head just might spin around like in a cartoon character! I started to feel myself get upset. I wanted to yell at her to stop her behavior, but I knew that wouldn't do any good.

Then I had a remembrance of a principle that changed everything. I remembered a lesson I learned from Brandon about the importance of managing my state of mind and how I could change my state by moving my body. So, I stopped in the midst of my anger and started doing jumping jacks.

At first, I was doing angry, jumping jacks, but after a short time, I was actually smiling. It was, after all, difficult to stay angry when I was tired and out of breath! I looked over at my daughter, who had gone from screaming to looking up at me in disbelief. Then she did something completely unexpected. She got up off the floor and started doing jumping jacks with me! Soon we were both laughing, and it changed the course of our entire day.

That moment in time stood out for me because it helped me to realize the power of leading by example. We can't force others to do what we want, but we can empower them to be their best by striving to be our best.

Prosperity Quadrant

I often struggled with feeling like I was a bad person. I have done a lot of good things in my life, and I try really hard to be a good person, but there are times when I find myself thinking negative or unkind thoughts.

Sometimes, I got stuck in those thoughts and allowed them to pull me down. I wanted to make more money, but I didn't know how, and there was a part of me that was afraid that I would always struggle financially. I wanted to create a better relationship with my husband, but I was so frustrated a lot of the time and was stuck in blaming him for the turmoil in our relationship.

I wanted to be a loving mom, but when crap hit the fan, and my kids were smearing feces on my bathroom walls and melting my carpet with a hairdryer, I felt like losing it and yelling at them.

I felt stuck in the patterns of my life that I desperately wanted to break free from, but I was trapped by them. I wanted to create a different life, but I didn't know how, and I didn't know if I even had it within myself to do it. I worried that I just didn't have what it takes.

I was listening to personal development CDs, and many were telling me to think positively and use affirmations (which is saying positive things about yourself), but it felt weird, and I didn't really feel much different after I did these things. I worried that something was wrong with me. Why couldn't I just overcome the negative part of myself that was holding me back?

I will never forget the day I looked at a sketch of the Prosperity Quadrant that Brandon had drawn. It seemed simple enough, and at first, I didn't understand it. It was a few days later that I was thinking about a couple I was coaching who were having relationship challenges with intimacy. I stopped for a moment and glanced down that the drawing of that principle— the Prosperity Quadrant—scribbled on a scrap piece of paper, and that is when it hit me like a ton of bricks.

I saw clearly how this principle helped make sense of why sometimes we feel stuck, or angry, or like we can't do something.

It made sense of why, we at times, feel like it is too hard to start and that we don't want to try. It made sense of why sometimes we feel hope and sometimes despair. It made sense of when we get in arguments with people we love and why we don't have the money we want. It made sense of it all. I began to understand why this one principle would change everything and why I needed to fully understand it, so I could break myself free from the things that were holding me back. I became aware that it was a major piece of the puzzle to having more money, passionate relationships, and happiness in this life.

The principle that brought all of these things to light for me was something that Brandon calls the Prosperity Quadrant. When you understand it and start to use it in your life, it will set you free.

Prosperity Quadrant

Let's dive into exactly what the Prosperity Quadrant is and how you can use it. The top "P" in the Prosperity Quadrant stands for a poor mindset, the bottom "M" stands for middle-class mindset, the "R" on the top right side of the quadrant stands for rich mindset, and the "A" on the bottom right stands for abundant mindset. So, what does all of that mean?

It means that how we experience the world and opportunities that are put in front of us are all dependent on our mindset. Our mindset colors absolutely everything in this life.

If we are having a good day or a bad day, if we think we can, or we can't. Everything we do, say, and experience is filtered through our mindset.

To understand how true this is, let me tell you a story. I recall interviewing the world-renowned artist Amy Segami. Amy specializes in Contemporary Suminagashi paintings, an ancient Chinese art form that was not practiced or well-known until Amy made a life-changing discovery.

You see, many people told Amy that the art form could not be done. Suminagashi is the process of dropping tiny drops of paint, which, when they connect with the water, disperse into beautiful circular rings. Many people would attempt to capture the colorful rings by placing paper onto the water but could never do so successfully. They told Amy it could not be done and discouraged her from trying.

Amy, however, had a different mindset about the artform. She had a background in engineering and understood the dynamics of water. Amy knew that the reason no one could capture the perfect circles was that the environment changed as the wind created by the paper approached the water. Then turbulence was created by the paper touching the surface of the water. Instead of seeing the colorful circles as the only thing worth capturing, she saw beauty in the chaos. Incredible images appeared to her in the water, not in spite of the turbulence but because of it. She captured the painting on the water on her paper and shared these images with the world.

What does Amy's story teach us about mindset? Everyone told Amy that what she wanted to do could not be done and that the images she saw in the water were not wanted. Amy had a mindset open to possibilities.

She saw the beauty in the imperfection, the story in the chaos, and then worked diligently to capture it to share with others.

You can hear Amy's interview and the stories of other incredible women on the My Fire Within Radio podcast.

So how does that apply to the prosperity quadrant? Well, when we are in a poor mindset, we are in a state of scarcity. There is not enough time, money, energy. We can't do it; it won't work out. We think of all the excuses and reasons why we can't. We often are stuck in a blame game of thinking that things aren't working because it is everyone else's fault. We are paralyzed in despair and inaction.

When we are in a middle-class mindset, we are settling for mediocrity. Things are just "fine," so we don't want to rock the boat. Things aren't painful enough to motivate us to change. This is a dangerous place to be in because this is where, in relationships, couples become roommates.

This is the mindset when we think it is too hard to change things, so why bother trying. We wait out a disconnected marriage until the kids grow because it is easier than fighting for the marriage. We just keep spending money we don't have and getting into debt because it is too hard to figure out another way to manage the money, and we don't want the Joneses to leave us in the dust. We stay in our dead-end day job even though we feel inspired to live our purpose, but we don't try because we are afraid of failing. We sit back on the couch of mediocrity.

The rich mindset is when we are really awesome at one aspect of life. An example of this is when the business owner is making millions of dollars but has a terrible marriage.

Or the mom is rocking being a parent but has no connection with her husband. Or the gigolo is fantastic in bed but has never had a lasting relationship. We are stuck being good at one part of life but let the rest of life fall by the wayside.

The Abundant Mindset is when we strive to create the life we want. We know it is not easy to change things, but we are willing to make daily strides to create the change we want. We take responsibility for our lives and do all we can to learn how to change it for the better. We seek mentors to help us learn how to do something we desire. We are humble, teachable, and open to feedback. When we make mistakes, we get back up fast. We are the first to apologize. We know that we don't need to be perfect, but we do need to be perfectly striving.

Now that you know the different mindsets in the Prosperity Quadrant, what does this have to do with you and being able to create the life you want? Well, we need to know and understand the Prosperity Quadrant because we all get stuck in different mindsets in different areas of our lives, and we need to see it for what it is and make a decision to move to a more abundant mindset. These mindsets are not stagnant, they are constantly moving, and we need to know if we are slipping into a poor mindset in our relationship so we can do something about it and move towards an abundant mindset!

When we know what to watch out for in the different mindsets, it is like taking the blinders off. We know that it is normal to slide back sometimes, but if we are aware of the warning signs, we can just get back up and do the next thing to move towards an abundant mindset. The most incredible thing is that Prosperity Quadrant applies to every single area of life. These mindsets show up in our relationships with the people we love the most; they show up in our financial results, they show up in the bedroom with intimacy.

They are always there. They are either helping us or hurting us, and we get to choose which it is.

There are three ingredients that we need to have in our lives to create the abundance we desire in all areas of life. All three of these must be present if you are to achieve abundance.

The first ingredient is that we need to know how to win from within. That is why I spent the majority of this book, giving you the knowledge and tools you need to win from within—so you have the capacity and character to create the life you want.

The second ingredient that we need is optimal health. This is essential because optimal health equals optimal energy, and we need energy to do anything in life! If we don't have the energy to do the work we want to do, play with our kids, or be present with our partner, this will drastically affect our results.

The third ingredient that we need to have is a financial vehicle. This vehicle will create the prosperity we desire. The financial vehicle can be our business, job, real estate, or other investments. It just needs to be a vehicle that aligns with the Four Keys of Business that I will cover in an upcoming chapter. This vehicle has to reliably and predictably help us achieve the financial results we desire.

For example, if you can win from within and have optimal health, you will have the character and energy you need to create the life you want. But you may experience financial stress—that will impact your health and relationships. If you have optimal health and a financial vehicle, you risk losing your relationships if you can't manage your state of mind with the people you love. If you can win from within and have a great financial vehicle but don't have optimal health, you won't have the energy you need to create lasting results in your relationships. Financially, you will be vulnerable to losing what you do have to sickness.

The incredible thing is that when we know what we need to do to move to and stay in an abundant manner, our entire life changes because we become able to create even more of the purpose, prosperity, and passion that we want in our life.

Opportunities Filtered

The opportunities we see and follow through on are filtered through our mindset.

We decide what we can and cannot do by what we believe is possible. I remember many times my mentor telling me about real estate deals that he would find so easily. He often said, "The deal of the decade comes around every week." Whenever I heard this, I thought, *well, not for me it doesn't!* I had created this block in my mind that I don't get deals and guess what...I didn't!

It wasn't until I started to change my focus to, *how can I get a great deal?* And was willing to put in the work required to find the deal that I was able to create over $20,000 in one day. You see, our mindset is what gives us the ability to get started and the motivation to keep going when it feels like it is too hard.

I have watched my mindset hold me back from doing what I really wanted to do, and I have watched myself push through even when it felt like all the odds were stacked against me. The thing we need always to remember, though, is that all opportunities, whether it is with your kids, your business, or your partner, are all filtered through our mindset. Are we open to seeing ourselves as empowered women who can create the life we want, or do we see ourselves as victims?

It is absolutely normal to slip into an unhelpful mindset. Believe me, I am an expert at it! But the thing we need to know with every part of our being is that we don't have to stay there! We can choose to see things in a new way; we can get back up and try again.

That is, after all, how we learn, how we are stretched, and how we gain the character needed to push through all the hard things to get to the good.

Where Opportunities are Found

Brandon said this one sentence to me years ago, and it has stuck with me in every single context of my life. The sentence that I go to when I am feeling overwhelmed, or stuck, or caught up in the chaos of life is this, "Opportunities are found in the present."

What does this really mean? It means that when we are stuck in our heads, or worried about the future, or feeling guilty about the past; we cannot see the opportunities that lie in front of us. It is like they are covered up, and the doorknob is not accessible to us.

I remember one day when I picked up the phone, and there was a woman from a popular news station on the other end of the line asking if Andy and I could do an interview about relationships with them the next day. "Of course," I said. I said yes without having an exact idea about what we were going to talk about in that interview.

The station was four hours away, so it would require driving up with my three kids and jumping onto the set with next to no time to prepare.

This was the first interview I had ever done, and I was terrified. So, we worked like crazy, getting together an outline of our talk, picked out the perfect outfit, and organized our family to go on this unexpected trip. I had confirmed that the show was an hour-long, and I thought that we would be interviewed for the entire hour. That is what we had prepared for.

Then we got to the news station, were standing in the green room, and found out that we had 15 minutes on air for the interview. We found this out just before going on air!

My heart skipped a beat! How on earth were we going to condense an hour of interview content into just 15 minutes?

They moved us into the waiting area on set, and we couldn't talk because they were filming. Andy and I mimed and wrote our suggestions on how to tackle the interview, and then we were up.

At that moment, I could have easily been washed over by my anxiety and uncertainty, but I stood in the moment and moved forward with faith that it would all work out.

After a very sincere plea to the Creator to help us out and a few deep breaths, we took the stage and guess what…it worked out! The interview was incredible, and we were fully engaged with the interviewers. In fact, they asked us back for another interview!

Why do I tell you that story? I tell you because life is not perfect. When an opportunity comes our way, it often feels like it's not the right time, that we don't have enough energy, and we are not sure it will work out. However, when we step forward with trust and do our best to step into the moment, we can fully engage in that opportunity, and although it is not always perfect, it is always worth it.

Digging Deep

Which mindset are you in most often?

What is one thing you could do to move toward an even more

abundant mindset? What is one thing you can do to be even more present?

CHAPTER 8:
THE FIVE EXTINGUISHERS OF FIRE

"Done is better than perfect." ~Sheryl Sandberg

Extinguisher of Fire #1 – Self-Doubt

TO UNDERSTAND SELF-DOUBT, we need to understand how exactly it stops us.

One of the biggest challenges of self-doubt is that we don't see it coming and don't even realize it is there when it arrives. We allow self-doubt to enter our mind by entertaining negative thoughts about ourselves and allowing them to stay. Thoughts like *I can't do this*; *I'm stupid*, or, *how could I have screwed up again,* accumulate and block our ability to move forward. They keep us stuck in the dangerous place of inaction.

However, when we understand this, we can move forward even though these negative thoughts that accumulate into a wall of self-doubt are before us. There is something we can do to break through the wall of self-doubt.

We can be valiant! When we are valiant, we move forward towards our goal even when we don't have it all figured out, even when we feel like we can't do it.

It is only through taking action that we get enough momentum to create results. When we are stuck in procrastination or self-doubt, our minds are busy coming up with all the reasons and excuses why we can't do it, and why we are destined to fail. Intentional action that we take toward our goals is the only way to quiet our self-doubt demons. In action, we don't have time to ask if we can do it or not.

There are times in this journey, however, when we will be met with uncertainty. We may, at times, try and fail. We may feel discouraged about our efforts that are not working as quickly as we want them to. We may feel alone in our trying to succeed. We may feel like it's not worth the effort.

In those moments, we must understand something. We must understand this because that discouragement that we feel can either drag us down to the depths of inactivity and despair or move us forward in faith and action. It can steal our dreams or empower us to light a fire within us that is so great that it can overcome anything put in our path.

As Neil A. Maxwell says, "Discouragement is not the absence of adequacy, but the absence of courage." So, let's not allow the absence of courage to enter our lives and our dreams. Let's not delay finding the courage within us to powerfully move forward and take the next step towards what we desire to achieve. There is courage that lies within you. More courage than you can possibly imagine. It is waiting to be set free in the small, consistent actions that you will take towards what you desire. So, take a step.

As we are in alignment with the Four Primary Laws of Fire and we take consistent, small steps towards our goals, our self-doubt becomes replaced with the courage and strength that comes from action.

When we are in action, there is no room for doubt. After all, we can't doubt what we have already done. It is through this process that we can doubt our doubts and create real results.

I have faced self-doubt many times in my life. It appeared one day when I was the sole organizer for an event, something I had never done before and didn't know how to do. I brought together three international speakers who would be presenting.

I was a stay at home mom most of the time and was working part-time in my business. The space between dropping off my daughter at preschool and picking her up again less than two hours later was my only time to work on this daunting project. I recall thinking so many times *I can't do this*. Sometimes the hardest thing I would accomplish in my tiny windows of work was to overcome these thoughts of self-doubt.

About two weeks before the event, I had a grand total of 14 people registered for my auditorium sized room. I panicked. How would I possibly be able to pull off this event when I was already proving that I couldn't do it?

My self-doubt became louder. I had nightmares of standing on the stage to announce the speakers only to look out on an empty auditorium with a few guests seated in the front row. I eventually got to the point of no return. A point when I realized that I couldn't do it on my own but that maybe the Creator knew how I could do it and could help me. I aligned with the Four Primary Laws of Fire and just kept taking the next step forward. I made sure that before I called anyone, I asked the Creator for help and gave up my self-doubt, insecurity, and fears.

I managed my state of mind by getting up out of my chair and moving my body. I focused on how I could truly serve the person I was talking to and asked the Creator for help to do so.

I stayed in growth by being willing to fail and realizing that although it was not comfortable, it is an important part of growth. I kept taking small, consistent steps toward filling the room every day in the time I had.

Doing this changed everything and allowed me to go from having 14 people registered for the event to a packed auditorium within a 2-week period. I still remember the roar of the crowd. What changed?

I changed. Even though I didn't know how to do it, even though I was scared and unsure, even though I had self-doubts, I did it anyway. I took the next step, did the next right thing, got up when I fell flat on my face. This experience taught me that we cannot be paralyzed by the walls of doubt when we are busy in action.

Momentum disempowers doubt.

Extinguisher of Fire #2 - Guilt

If we are not careful, guilt can keep us stuck in our past mistakes or paralyzed with fear about our future ones.

We feel guilty about not being the perfect mom, the most loving wife, not feeding our family homecooked meals every day of the week that are perfectly balanced for optimum health. We feel guilty when we are working. We feel guilty when we are not working. We feel guilty when we are working out because our kids have to wait for our attention. We feel guilty when we are not working out. It is enough to drive anyone crazy!

It is so insidious because when we make a mistake and feel guilty about it, it keeps us stuck in that mistake. That is dangerous because then we can't learn from it. We are stuck dwelling on things that have already happened that we cannot change. This stops our growth and keeps us from moving on. It is not helpful or healthy!

We can also be unable to move on from guilt for what we haven't done yet. Guilty about the awards we haven't achieved, the wealth we haven't accumulated, the mistakes we likely will make with our kids.

This is a sneaky snare because it keeps us focused on future anxiety and prevents us from being in the moment, which incidentally is the only place change can happen.

Guilt Can Motivate You or Keep You Stuck

Even though we all experience guilt to some degree or another, we need to understand that it is not all bad. Guilt can keep us stuck, or it can empower us to move forward to create the changes we want in our lives.

Sometimes it can be the very thing that tells us that something is off that we need to fix. The difference between guilt that immobilizes us and guilt that moves us forward is how long we stay in it. Are we stuck dwelling on our guilty feelings, or are we motivated to make a change for the better, learn from our mistakes, and move on?

That is the sweet spot where guilt can help bring out our best character, help us learn from our mistakes, and encourage us to grow constantly.

You don't need to stay stuck in guilt. You can recognize the feeling and move on towards creating your best self.

I can talk about guilt so thoroughly because I have become a wee bit of an expert on the topic. You see, if guilt was a town, I would have a vacation home there. I have spent a lot of time in guilt and tend to feel guilty about it and well, everything.

There is, however, one lesson I have discovered that has helped me to learn from my mistakes and let go of guilt faster than ever before. In fact, it is something that helps me move from guilt to an empowering state of mind in just moments. It is crazy how effective it is.

The lesson I learned is that we cannot stay in guilt and gratitude at the same time. There is always something to be grateful for in every situation. Sometimes it takes a lot of digging, but it is there. I realized that when I feel guilty about something, I can move past the guilt by asking myself what I am grateful for until I find an answer. There is a lesson to be learned in everything.

For example, I feel guilty when people help me sometimes. I don't want to put them out, and I feel like I should be able to do it all by myself. There was this one time when one of my friends invited me to the movies with my family. I really wanted to go, but at the time, our finances were really tight, so we didn't have the extra money to go.

When I explained the situation to my friend, she said, "Well, the movie is more fun with the Benjamin family, so the movie is on us." I felt so guilty that my friend was paying for our tickets. I started to go into scheming mode about how I would get the money, so she didn't have to pay for us.

I called my friend and told her thanks for offering to pay for our tickets, but I found money so she wouldn't need to pay for us. She told me that she wanted to buy our tickets. I felt so guilty.

Then I realized that the guilt I was feeling was keeping me from experiencing gratitude for the kindness and generosity of my friend. If I could be grateful for her gift, wouldn't I be more able to enjoy the movie and my friendship?

So that is what I did. I became really grateful, and it completely changed my experience. I have done this, many times over, and when I feel guilty about a mistake I have made or guilty that I am not where I feel like I "should" be in life, I look for what I could be grateful for, and it completely changes my perspective and my ability to experience joy.

Extinguisher of Fire #3 - Procrastination

If you are a living, breathing human being…which I can safely bet you are if you are reading this, then you sometimes procrastinate.

It is something that we all do. In fact, it is in our very nature to push anything that is hard to do to the future. If it is in our very nature to do this, then what's the big deal, right? The reality is that the most important things in this life are often hard to do.

Sometimes, we say, "I'll do that hard thing someday." Sounds like reasonable logic; however, most often, someday never comes. I have never seen a day in the week, month, or year marked "someday." As Marvin Ashton put it, "Procrastination is an unwholesome blend of doubt and delay."

When we procrastinate, we put off our goals and dreams for a later time that may never come. Usually, what gets put off are the things we want most in this life but are afraid of trying to achieve. So, what do we lose when we procrastinate? We can run out of time, lose blessings that we would have had, lose opportunities, or lose out on living our purpose.

But, if procrastination is such a dangerous thing, why on earth would we put ourselves through it? Well, there is a mindset that goes along with procrastination that lulls us into believing it is the best option. This mindset is empowered by a series of thoughts that our logical mind can hold onto to justify the delay. If we are not aware of this procrastination thinking, we will fall prey to it. Some of the thoughts that keep us procrastinating are; *it's too hard. It's too late. The task seems impossible,* or *I don't have enough (time, money, talent).*

One time I received a tax form that I needed to fill out. I don't know what it is about tax forms, but they kind of freak me out. I worry that I will fill them out wrong, or I will need a ton of information to dig up that I either don't have or don't know where to find and so I procrastinated filling it out. I put off filling out this form for months.

Finally, the deadline for completing the form was upon me, and so I grabbed the paper and reluctantly began filling it out. I made a goal to work on the form for 15 minutes every day until it was completed. I was shocked and a little embarrassed to find that once I actually put pen to paper, I filled out the form in just five minutes.

That's right; I sheepishly admit that it literally took me five minutes to fill out the form after months of procrastination. At that moment, I realized that procrastination takes up too much energy and time.

I finally understood that if I just took action on what I was afraid of one step at a time, I could accomplish more than I thought possible, without the guilt and worry!

To be able to break through procrastination and move towards creating the results we want, here are five elements to overcoming procrastination:

Desire – We need to genuinely want to do it. For example, we are not going to run a marathon if we have no desire to go running!

Thoughts – Our thoughts need to support the change we want to make. If we are constantly telling ourselves that we cannot do it, that will become true.

Plan – Next, we need to plan how we are going to make the change we want to make by breaking it down into simple, small, daily steps. I go through exactly how to do this in the goal-setting chapter of this book.

Action – The next step is to take small, consistent action! We will not change simply by thinking about it or planning it. This seems pretty basic, but I can't tell you how many entrepreneurs I have met who spend years planning to start their business but never actually starting it!

Be Valiant – The final step is being valiant. That means when we fall down or forget or procrastinate (which we will at times), we just get back up and try again.

When we follow these five elements to overcoming procrastination, we are given an added measure of strength, courage, wisdom, help from the Creator, and the ability to create lasting and meaningful change. We are able to achieve things that we didn't know were possible.

Extinguisher of Fire #4 - Pride

Pride causes nations to fall, marriages to fail, families to fall apart, and individuals to give up on themselves.

There are a few different ways we can experience pride. We can feel pride towards the Creator, the people around us and within ourselves. Pride towards the Creator comes out in many ways but can be summed up by a feeling of; *I want what I want when I want it.* It is an impatience for the things we desire in this life and a selfish willingness to put our own agenda ahead of what our Creator wants us to do. This type of pride can also appear when we cherry-pick Fire Principles. This is when we choose to align with only the Fire Principles that are easy to follow. It is really saying to our Creator, "I know better than you do."

The next type of pride is towards the people around us. It is not just a puffing-up feeling like we are better than someone, but it is so much more. Pride slips into our lives with destructive force when we judge others or have contention with others. Pride sneaks in even when we are looking upwards and judging someone.

This frequently happens in our society with "rich trash talk" in saying things like "They have so much money, why do they have such a big house?" The reality is that we have no idea about people's circumstances or hearts. The richest person living in a mansion on a hill might be giving more to those in need than the judgmental person living below. The other reality is that it is not our place to judge. Another way that pride creeps into relationships is through an unwillingness to apologize or make things right.

I remember one day being in the car with Andy, and we had an argument over something. There was palpable tension in the vehicle as we each sat drenched in silence with arms crossed and eyebrows furrowed. We sat in silence for most of the ride until he broke it by saying, "I would rather be happy than right. I'm sorry for my part in this, and I just want to be close to you. I love you."

This first step toward me began to soften my heart and allowed me to look within myself to find my part in the conflict. It wasn't long before I was apologizing, and a feeling of love filled our car again.

Pride prevents us from seeing the divine potential of others. It creates walls of judgment, scarcity, and fear between us and the people around us. It will damage relationships and our own hearts.

The last kind of pride is pride within us.

That is the pride of thinking we are better than other people. This pride is also found when we take full credit for our accomplishments and forget that all we have and all we are able to accomplish in this life is through the grace of our Creator.

The gifts we have and the talents we possess are given to us by a loving Creator who wants us to share them with others and grow our character. When we are in this pride, we forget our divine potential, and it is like spiritual blinders appear, causing us to be lost in lust for superficial things.

Pride Cycle

We need to understand that pride gets in the way of living a purposeful and passionate life and that the Creator loves us too much to let that happen. So, when we are stuck in an unhealthy pattern of pride, the Creator will help us move away from pride to become teachable by making life harder for us.

The Creator does this because, as Brandon says, the Creator "cares about our character more than he cares about our comfort." Then when we start losing things in our life, we become more willing to turn to the Creator. He gives us these challenges, so we will become teachable again to help us step into our divine potential. This is called the pride cycle, and we are always in one part of the pride cycle.

Pride Cycle

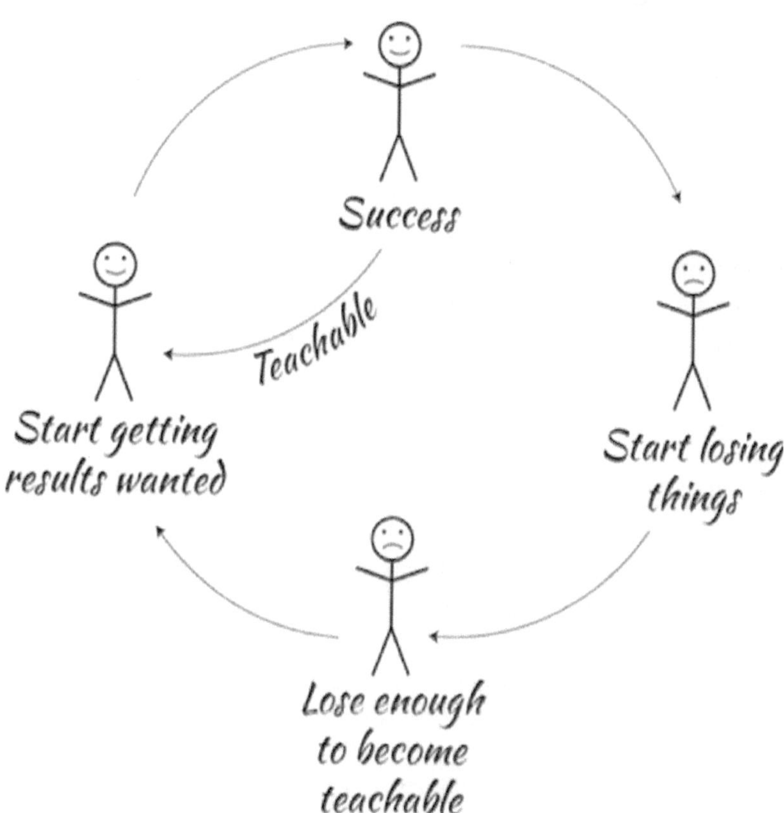

The good news is that we get to choose which part of the pride cycle we are in. We can wait for the Creator to help us become humble through challenges, or we can choose to stay teachable, humble, and grateful by aligning with the Four Primary Laws of Fire.

I have fallen into pride many times, and I can say from experience that it is much more pleasant to choose to align with the Four Primary Laws of Fire than having to go through challenges to help me let go of my pride.

Extinguisher of Fire #5: The Comparison Trap
One of the biggest dangers that threaten our success and the sense of

accomplishment we feel as we are working towards our goals is comparing ourselves to others.

This is dangerous because there will always be someone who is better skilled, better looking, or has more accomplishments in various areas of life. There are three parts to the comparison trap that can snare us. If we are not aware of them, we can become discouraged, overcome with self-doubt, and competitive and unsupportive of the women around us.

The comparison Trap often causes us to feel disappointed and critical of our physical appearance. We can feel disconnected from our family as we compare the seemingly perfect family images on Instagram. We can feel like we have failed ourselves and the Creator when we only look at the carefully crafted personas of famous people we admire. We can be left feeling like we don't measure up like we are a failure, and that everyone else has it all figured out.

Instead of feeling connected to other women, we can feel alone and like we need to wear a mask pretending to be someone we are not. We can fear that if people saw who we really are, they would not like what they see. We retreat into a life of regret, disappointment, and envy.

Being aware of the traps allows us to be set free from them so we can be focused on being the best version of ourselves and supporting others to do the same.

I used to compare myself to other people and feel guilty and ashamed that I wasn't as successful in the areas of life they were successful in. Then I realized that no one is perfect, there are things they are good at, and things they struggled with. There are things I am good at and things I struggle with.

The only person I need to compare myself with is the person I am now and who I want to become. Then I need to work my butt off to be that person.

Part 1: They Are Better at Everything

When we compare ourselves to others, we run the risk of assuming that because someone is better at one aspect of life than us, they are better in all aspects of life. However, the reality is that we are all just doing our best and striving to make daily improvements.

No one has it all figured out, nor are we supposed to! When we compare ourselves to others, we run the risk of lusting after what they have. This breaks the Fire Principle of Gratitude. When we are lusting after something, we aren't feeling grateful for what we already have. When we assume that they are better at everything, we miss opportunities to serve them in the area they need help with. No one is good at everything! Everyone has something they need to work on, and we all have gifts and talents to share.

If we understand this and we stop judging ourselves and others, we will see how we can help them in the areas they struggle in and will be open to receiving their help in the areas they excel in.

Part 2: It's Easy For Them

When we compare ourselves to others, it is easy to misunderstand what it took for them to achieve that result we long for. So often, we can assume that a person who is in great shape was just was born with great genetics.

However, while it's true that we all have different genetics and body types, people who are in great shape (not just thin but strong in mind, body, and spirit) have worked very hard to get there…and stay there.

Just think about the discipline required to plan for and eat healthy meals and snacks, to exercise vigorously and regularly. These are the things that need to be done consistently before anyone can get the result of a toned body. If we forget that and think they were born that way or it comes easier to them, we risk falling into hopelessness.

When we begin working toward a goal that is important to us, we become more likely to stop working toward our goals, when it gets hard or when we don't see the results right away. The reality is that everything worth doing takes work. In fact, as Angela Duckworth says, "Talent counts, effort counts twice." This saying helps us understand that we don't need natural talent to succeed. It is more important for us to have the determination to focus on consistent improvement.

I did not have this mentality when I fell into the comparison trap when I was trying to be healthier by working out, and after five sessions of sweat and a few tears, I looked at the beautiful, perfectly sculpted instructor and thought, *I've been working my butt off, and I still have curves in all the wrong places. What's the point? I'll never look like that anyway!* I felt like quitting with some lame excuse like, "The program wasn't for me."

Then I realized that the instructor had to work out many times before she got to where she is at. I began to understand that I am where I am, and there is no shame in that, but if I want to change the results I currently have, I need to try something different.

I started telling myself; *I am getting stronger and more able to do the workouts every day. If I keep doing this, I will get results.* I became more motivated to do the workouts every day, even when I didn't see results. Months later, my body shifted, and I found abs underneath my muffin top, and I got stronger and had more energy.

I realized that to achieve anything I want in this life; I need to take action first to create results and then have the patience and diligence necessary to wait until the result I want is achieved.

Part 3: What Do They Think About Me?

Another reason the comparison trap is dangerous is that it keeps us focused on ourselves. When we are feeling self-conscious, it is often because we are comparing our successes or our feeling that we lack success to others. If we feel self-conscious about our weight, for example, we might stand in a way that makes us look less heavy with our belly sucked in.

This self-consciousness prevents us from reaching our full potential and aligning with the Four Primary Laws of Fire because it keeps us focused on ourselves! If we are so busy being preoccupied with trying to look skinnier or worried about what others will think about us, we are not managing our state of mind, and so we are not present.

When we are not present, we can't see opportunities that are in front of us and so we miss opportunities to serve those around us. Have you ever been in a conversation where you are so worried about how you look or what the other person will think of you that you can't remember what the other person just said? I have! How can we connect with the people around us and truly listen to them if we are worried about how we look or what they will think about us? The times I have just let go of worrying about what I look like and focus all of my energy on being present with the person in front of me is when I can truly serve them.

Another incredible thing happens when we let go of being self-conscious and focus on serving; we feel better about ourselves and are less self-conscious! When I first started doing this, it was difficult, and I needed to practice not sucking in my belly. I would say to myself: *I am where I am, and that is okay. Today is going to be a fantastic day.* If I still had difficulty focusing on the other person rather than on all my flaws, I would pray for help to be able to let go of the self-consciousness and receive the knowledge I needed to help the person in front of me.

I was asked to do an interview on a large tv network, and I was so nervous. I looked in the mirror and saw every flaw in my complexion; I tried on the dress I would be wearing and assessed whether or not my muffin top would be showing up to the interview if I sat down. I looked up the people who would be interviewing me so I could be more effective during the interview, and my anxiety grew as I looked at these beautiful women with impeccable makeup and slender bodies. As you can likely guess at this point, I was comparing myself to them…and I was not measuring up.

I recall walking into the news station. I had done the best I could with my makeup, but let's just say that cosmetology is not my strong suit. I wasn't too worried about it because I was sure a makeup artist would touch up my face with a little makeup CPR.

I was sitting in the green room waiting to be called on stage when a beautiful woman with these perfectly contoured eyes glided over and asked if I had any questions. I asked if I could see the makeup artist before going on set. That is when she let me know that there was no makeup artist, but she was sure I looked just fine.

A wave of panic flooded over me as I did a mental checklist, asking myself if my makeup looked crazy.

I didn't want to allow my pride to get in the way of serving the people I could help through the interview. So, I decided right then and there that I would do all I could to look my best and then I would forget the rest. Forget my self-consciousness. Forget about my muffin top. Forget about my feelings of inadequacy. I would fill my heart and mind with a desire to serve, and I would ask for help from the Creator so I could do it.

Once I did that, it was incredible how I felt so free to be present during the interview. I could be myself and appreciated the people I was with more, and I was even able to have fun!

The interview was an incredible success, and I got to stay and hang out with the interviewers, and they wanted my husband and me to come back on the show.

In fact, after the interview, we got asked to coach the next person going on set about how to give a great interview.

Steps to Let Go of Comparing

Through these experiences, I have learned that there are tried and true things we can do to let go of comparing ourselves to others so we can be truly present.

These things work when I am on TV interviews; they work when I'm on stage; they work when I am working out with other moms. They just work.

Step One: Ask for help from the Creator to let go of your self-consciousness, or other feelings that are holding you back like guilt, shame, fear, or worry. Ask for help to truly connect with the person in front of you.

Step Two: Tell yourself things that build you up. How we talk to ourselves matters! No more talk about, *I look fat*, or, *I'm a loser!* Replace negative thoughts with thoughts that build you up like *I am where I am and where I am is okay!* Or, *I am beautiful*, or, *I am loving and present.*

Step Three: Focus on being present with and serving the other person. When you focus on the other person, you will be able to let go of your feelings of self-consciousness, and you will be able to truly be present with the other person.

You will hear what is important to them and why, and you will be able to help them. Sometimes just really being present with someone is the best way to serve them. It is also the best way to have influence.

As Theodore Roosevelt said, "People don't care how much you know until they know how much you care." They will know how much you care when you are willing to be uncomfortable (by letting go of your feelings of self-consciousness) in order to be truly present with them.

Stop comparing yourself to others! As Jordan Peterson says, "If you want to compare yourself to someone, compare yourself to who you were yesterday and get better and better every day!" You are beautiful and awesome, just the way you are! You don't have to be perfect to be wonderful. You don't have to be perfect to be able to have influence and to help people. You don't have to be a size 6 to be a leader. You don't have to have the perfect body for people to love you.

You are where you are and where you are is more than okay! It is also true that you are not done with being your best self and that you have the power to get even better.

As you go through this book, I will walk you through the steps to create the results you want. Starting where you're at is exactly where you are supposed to start.

If you would like more support overcoming the Comparison Trap, go to www.myfirewithin.com/resources and grab your free spot in the My Fire

Within Class.

Now you have it…the extinguishers to your inner fire. You know how the extinguishers of firework and understand how to prevent the extinguishers of fire from snuffing out your inner flame.

Let's talk about the accelerant that fuels your fire within. This accelerant is being able to change your beliefs. When we know how to change our beliefs, our inner potential can be unleashed because we are no longer held back by the shackles of limiting beliefs.

As Jordan Peterson says, "If you want to compare yourself to someone, compare yourself to who you were yesterday and get better and better every day!"

Igniting the Fire

Now that we understand some of the pitfalls that can keep us stuck and prevent us from living a life with fire, we need to know how to change our beliefs in a powerful way, so we fan the flame of the fire within us.

There are three things that are most effective in changing what we believe is possible. I used to think it was impossible to change my beliefs, but then I started using these three steps to igniting the fire, and I realized that not only is it possible, predictable. It works every time. As we change our beliefs, we free ourselves from the chains that hold us back.

The three steps to igniting the fire are:
- proximity
- repetition
- experience

Step One: Proximity. Proximity means being around people who have the beliefs and the results that you want.

Beliefs are supported and reinforced by the stories we tell ourselves about our lives and about the lives of others we connect with. When we change the stories that surround us, we change what we believe is possible for us and for others.

In doing so, we open up opportunities that were invisible to us before.

Our stories lead us toward our destiny. When we are with people who have stories of the results we want to create, we see that it is possible, and we start to understand that we can do it too.

I created My Fire Within Radio so you can hear the real and raw stories of incredible women as they share their expertise as well as their individual journeys when navigating work, relationships, and the chaos of life.

I love that these field leaders, best-selling authors, and mompreneurs reveal their secrets to success, share when they felt like giving up, and reveal what helps them to juggle family, work, and everything in between.

Their stories uplift me, encourage me to keep going, and help me not to feel alone.

You can hear their life-changing stories on the My Fire Within Radio podcast.

Step Two: Repetition. Repetition means that we change our beliefs by telling ourselves new stories over and over until we believe them.

I used to think that affirmations were not effective until I did an exercise called the Dream Page, and I started seeing results skyrocket in my life. I started making more money, was calmer with my kids, and felt less stressed and more focused.

If you miss a day, no problem, you just start back at day one. This repetition allows the new beliefs that you want in your life to become part of the norm for you. You begin to see your life the way you want to create it. It truly is powerful and effective.

My real-life experiences have been verified by breaking science. Researchers have discovered that people with chronic negative thoughts have different brain architecture than people who are success oriented.

Step Three: **Experience**. Experience means that as we take steps forward and do things, even when we feel like we are not up to the task, our beliefs change based on what we have actually accomplished. We can no longer tell ourselves that we can't eat healthy when we are eating healthy. Facts change beliefs. To start this process, you just need to take the next step.

I know that as we shift our understanding of who we are, and we take steps toward creating the life we desire, we step into our potential. We become greater than we knew possible. As we educate our desires toward a higher standard of love and compassion toward ourselves and others, we begin to want to do more of what brings us closer to the people we love, the Creator, and to the best version of ourselves.

Digging Deep

What is one thing you can do to feel grateful more often?

What is one step you can take toward working on a task you are avoiding?

If you would like support with knowing your next step to overcoming the extinguishers of fire, book a discovery call with a Fire Within Coach at www.myfirewithin.com/resources.

CHAPTER 9:
SECRET #3 BALANCE WITH FIRE

"Never get so busy making a living that you forget to make a life." ~Dolly
Parton

Priorities With F.I.R.E.
I THINK WOMEN HAVE BEEN TOLD a lie that tears us apart inside.

It is one that keeps us from taking care of ourselves and making a huge difference in the world. It is one that breaks apart families and dreams. We have been told that we have to choose. We need to choose between taking care of ourselves and being a good mother. We have been told that we have to choose between having an awesome family and making a difference in this world.

When we feel like we have to choose between our family and our purpose, we can feel stressed, overwhelmed, and like there is a tug-of-war within us. It can cause us to feel disconnected from our husbands and kids. This tug of war can prevent us from receiving inspiration from the Creator and halt our progression. We can feel like we can't win and feel disheartened.

I don't think we need to choose between our family and living our purpose through our work.
I think there is a way we can do everything we want in this life by doing things in the right order at the right time, with the right intent.

But we cannot do it all at once. This is what Women With Fire do. We know we need to light ourselves before lighting others. We hear all the time that we have to take care of ourselves before we can take care of others, but while this is true, it is often the exception rather than the rule.

Why is it so hard to do this in real life? It's hard to do because women have a natural tendency to put everyone's needs ahead of our own. It's hard to do because we get lost in the chaos of life and overwhelmed by our "to do" list. It's hard to do because it is likely that no one ever showed us how. I love how Michelle Obama puts it, that "We need to do a better job of putting ourselves higher on our own 'to do' list."

The first thing we need to understand is that we do not have a time management problem; we have a priority problem! Putting our priorities in the right order is the first step to balancing everything without losing our minds.

I used to feel like I couldn't be successful in my work and be present with my family, but then I learned a lesson that helped me understand that I can be successful at both. I learned that I could hit targets at work and with my family in small bursts of time and that if I put did things in priority, I could accomplish more than I ever thought possible.

Before I dive into how to put our priorities in order so we can achieve all that we want in this life, I need to be super real about something.

Completely balancing our priorities is a myth. It is not possible to perfectly balance all the roles and priorities that we have at the same time. Balancing our work and our life is more like Chinese plate spinning.

I first heard this example from David Bednar. You know, those beautiful images of women juggling several spinning plates on the end of long sticks? When we have different priorities in our lives, it is like each priority is a plate. At first, when we take on that priority, it takes a lot of energy to get the plate spinning, and as we add more plates, it becomes more difficult to spin them at the same time.

All of the plates need us to keep spinning them one at a time. If we stop spinning them, they fall. Priorities are like that. We can't spin all our priority plates at the same time, they all need us to spin them just briefly one at a time, and if we take on too many plates, it becomes difficult to spin all of them, and one will likely fall. We also need to understand that the bigger the plate is, the more energy that will be required to spin the plate. This is why it is critical to breaking our priorities down into smaller, more manageable activities.

For example, the goal to feel more connected with my kids is pretty big and vague, but the goal of creating one pure moment per day with each of my kids—now, that I can do! I love this example so much because it helps me remember that having peace with our priorities just requires us to be clear about what priorities are most important to us and that we have a way to spin that priority in small, consistent ways. In this next section, I am going to share with you how to identify what priorities are most important, which priorities you need to spin first and help the rest spin more easily.

The first step in getting our priorities in an order that will empower us as women is that we need to see just how out of whack our priorities really are. In our society, most women naturally tend to prioritize in the following way: We put our kids first, then everyone else, then our partner, then

FINALLY, ourselves.

This way of managing our priorities is not happy; it's not healthy, nor is it productive. By the time we finish with our kids, we struggle to plaster a smile on our face for the world. Then we expend what little energy we have left with our partner (not well, might I add), and we end up with less than nothing left for ourselves.

Notice that I didn't even mention the Creator... because in our overwhelm, the Creator is often forgotten. We feel alone at the very time we need the Creator the most! Can you see how this pattern leaves us feeling empty, overwhelmed, resentful, and frustrated?

How then do we put our priorities in an order that builds us up and empower us to be our best selves? Brandon taught me about principles, and it was a turning point in my life that helped me feel more peace, more connected to the people I love, and more effective in achieving my goals.

What is the order of priorities that brings us closer to purpose, prosperity, and passion? This order is not about political correctness or the fad of the day. It is instead an order that ensures that we have the energy to be our best...our best at home, and in our work! This order will sound simple, but it truly makes all the difference.

Like a series of lenses, when priorities line up in the right order, the energy that goes out in the world is like a magnified light...transforming from warm passive energy to laser intensity.

Let's take some time exploring these relationships in detail.

The most effective way to have our priorities in order is to have F.I.R.E. Priorities.

First Creator - Connect with the Creator
Inspired Self Care - care for yourself physically and emotionally
Relationship with Partner - Connect with your partner
Engage Children - Connect with your children

F - First You

We need to do an activity before noon that strengthens us physically and emotionally. We cannot give what we do not have, so as Women With Fire, we need to stoke our fire first!

One of the most misunderstood concepts in our society is the idea of putting ourselves first. What does this mean? To put yourself first really means doing things that will lift you up and fill you with energy. I am not talking about the surface self-care of manicures and cucumber scrubs that we see in the movies. Although those things are great, it is not what I am talking about here.

Taking care of yourself means doing things that inspire your best self and lift and strengthen you like working out, meditating, asking yourself empowering questions. These things will help you to be your best self and have the energy to be who you want to be for everyone else. This will also help you connect with the Creator so you can receive inspiration about your life and your goals.

Too often, when we want to make a change in our life, we seek Divine help from a place of scarcity and fear.

We plead for what we want, like a spoiled child wailing for a new toy. When we are in this kind of state of mind, we are not open to receiving help from the Divine and cannot hear the guidance we are being given. Taking care of ourselves physically and emotionally puts us in a frame of mind to hear the guidance of the Heavenly Guide.

I – Inspiration

Seeking for connection with the Creator will help us to receive inspiration about our purpose, how we can increase our prosperity, and how we can create passionate and loving relationships.

As Brandon says, "If we lean on things bigger than this world, then nothing in this world can stop us." Think about this for a moment. If we start our day being a team with our Creator, how much more help will we get throughout our day? How much more lifted and strengthened will we be to remember that we are not alone when life gets crazy?

It is easy to be swept up in our to-do lists and the needs of others. However, if we want to have the energy we need, there is no other way! Different people accomplish this in different ways. Some women talk to the Creator, pray, meditate, or read spiritual books. All that matters is that we find a way to connect with the Creator with a sincere intention.

R - Relationship with Partner

Making our relationship with our partner a priority allows us to face the rest of our life as a team and gives us tremendous strength. This means doing little things like saying good morning and kissing before you leave for work. Having this connection will not only help you feel more loved, but it will also help your kids feel more secure.

Research even shows that being connected with your partner will also help you make more money.[6]

One morning, I was in the kitchen washing dishes. Andy was heading off to work, and as he walked by me, I turned to say goodbye when suddenly, I remembered this principle. I rushed to meet him at the back door, grabbed him by the shirt collar, and kissed that boy within an inch of his life. He looked up at me with googly love eyes, and I knew I had his heart. Looking into my eyes, he said, "You are my favorite," then he went off to work with a little more strut in his step. We both had a more incredible day and were more effective in our work because we were connected and felt loved.

E - Engage Children

Create moments in the day where we can be present and loving with our children. The relationships with our kids are of eternal significance, and we need to treat them with the respect and love they deserve. This does not mean that you need to be a perfect mom. There is no such thing! It means striving to be your best self, getting back up when you make mistakes, and finding pure moments in the chaos of the day to be present and connect with your kids. These pure moments really don't take long. A hug, an "I love you," and playing for five minutes can make all the difference in helping our kids feel loved.

One day, when I was insanely busy with multiple deadlines looming over me, my kids kept coming into my office wanting to play. I felt the pressure of all that I needed to do, but I wanted my kids to feel loved. Then I remembered the Principle of Pure Moments, so I closed my computer, and as my kids were walking away, I reached my hands up high, turning them into monster hands and chased them around the house, tickling them.

My girls burst into fits of giggles as they looked back at me and ran through the house. It didn't take a long time to make that moment, and I was so grateful knowing that for just a few minutes, I had their hearts.

Fifth, and finally, is everyone else and our work. Now that we have put our most important priorities first, we have a greater capacity and strength to serve others because we have done things in the right order at the right time. This is when we can truly serve and accomplish great things in our work and build meaningful connections with our extended family and friends.

I know what you might be thinking. *How do we have these priorities in order in real life?* You know, when you're tired, the kids are sick, you have a big deadline in your work, or when you don't have enough time. I'll admit it can be messy, but it is possible.

The first thing you need to understand is that we put these priorities in place when everything has equal importance. For example, if you haven't connected with your partner yet, but your child hurt herself. You help your child first and then connect with your partner.

The other thing you need to understand is that all of these priorities do not need to take a long time. An example of how priorities can be met quickly is saying a prayer when I wake up instead of checking my phone. I say, "I love you" to Andy instead of going to the kids right away. I give my kids a hug before picking up my phone. Then I can move on with the rest of my day.

When I started putting this into practice into my own life, it was a game-changer. I used to feel like I never had time to work out. I wanted to be healthier, but once the day rolled on, my workout never got in. When I realized that my priorities were out of balance and that I needed to start putting myself first, it was like a light switched on within me.

I set my alarm and woke up early to work out. Sometimes my kids were fighting in the background, and distractions would come up that would make it hard to keep going. I knew that I couldn't stop though, I had to take care of myself, so I could be healthy enough to watch my kids grow.

I have found that as I have done this, I have had more energy than ever before, more patience and love for my family, and I have more capacity to do work that I know will help women from around the world. At the moment, it doesn't seem like these small daily decisions will make a difference, but they make all the difference.

If you would like more support with overcoming the Balance Myth, you can hop on my free My Fire Within Class at www.myfirewithin.com/resources to learn about the lie society taught us about success.

Taking the Blinders Off

Now that you know how to have your priorities in the right order, you can move on to the next part of creating the life you want by becoming even more of who you want to be. To do this, you must first ask yourself, *who do I want to be?*

I remember a time in my life when I felt like I needed to do it all. I wanted to be a perfect mom, a loving and passionate partner, support my community and those in need, build a successful business, and have incredible relationships with all those around me. The mere thought of all this made me feel as though I was carrying a 1000-pound weight.

It was at this point I turned to my teacher and mentor for help. I explained that my heart was longing to be with my daughter as she grew up. I didn't want to miss anything, but I felt the weight of needing to provide for my family and the desire to serve those outside my family too. I felt like I was being pulled in so many different directions that I wasn't sure which way turn.

Then I was asked a question that allowed me to see clearly what I needed to do and what is truly important to me. The question was, "What three things are you not willing to live without?" That question seemed as though it pierced my soul as I pondered what I really was not willing to live without. What would be most important to me…so important that as I looked back over my life, I would know that I lived it well, that the most precious things were put first and that I did not miss out?

Suddenly the answer came to me, and I looked up with a knowing in my heart and said with complete confidence, "I am not willing to live without my Creator, living up to my full potential, and my husband and children." There it is…those are the things I will fight for in this life to have no matter what. So the journey began to align my life to the things that matter most and to the relationships I so desired to have.

It is one thing to become clear about the three things you are not willing to live without, and it is another thing entirely to change your life to create it. At the point in my life, when I made this decision to put my three things first, we were in debt close to $100,000, and we're in the hole $1200 each month.

I was stressed out, feeling empty and frustrated in my job, and I felt like I was a zombie going through the motions of my life.

I felt as though I couldn't possibly create the life I wanted when I was so busy being stuck in survival mode with no time to even think about what that life might look like, let alone create it.

I decided that I wanted to work from home part-time and be a stay at home mom, but I felt so guilty that Andy would be mostly responsible for financially providing for our family. This was scary for me. We were not "making it" financially as a two-income family. I thought, *how on earth will I be able to provide for our family if I take a drastic pay cut?* To say this was a leap of faith would be a serious understatement!

At the time of this decision, Andy had a cushy government job with health care benefits and a pension. Sounds perfect, doesn't it? On paper, things looked good, but he was not finding joy in his work. He had this feeling screaming within him of wanting to do more, to help more, to be more.

Both of us felt the nudge of the Creator to move toward living our purpose, but we were not sure what that meant. Looking back at that moment in my life, amidst the chaos of creation and possibilities, I could not see that we were at a turning point that would change things forever. As Thomas S. Monson said, "The hinges of destiny turn on small hinges."

How true that is. I can look back now and see that the life we have created, living in the place of our dreams with palm trees, staying home with my kids to watch them grow, and replacing our 9-5 incomes so we could do what we really love to do all started because Andy and I reflected on a life-changing question and then created our life based on it.

Seasons with Fire

Do you ever feel sick and tired of everyone telling you that you can have it all?

I feel this way sometimes. In this world today, we are expected to do everything at the same time. Get married, have children, build a successful career or business, become a millionaire, save the world with charity work, get in shape…and the list goes on and on. It is exhausting!

I don't know about you, but every time I try to do everything all at the same time, life gets messy, stressful, and overwhelming. Usually, I don't get anyone thing done! When I am in this mode I feel like I am running on a treadmill and the treadmill is going faster and faster, and some jerk keeps increasing the hill size, and my feet can't keep up so I'm tripping and eventually I just fly off the treadmill and land in a heap on the floor.

What is the answer then? Is it possible to have it all? Can we really have incredibly connected relationships and build successful careers or businesses? Can we actually take care of ourselves and others without losing ourselves while we do it? Is it possible to find balance and peace while creating the life we want?

I used to feel like I couldn't have everything I want in life because when I tried to have everything, I failed at it all. Then I realized that I can have everything I want as long as I do my best to stay in priority. A couple of things have been game-changing in helping me have the balance and peace that I want, and I am so excited to share them with you so you can have everything that you want!

As women, we go through more seasons of life than men do. We go through the seasons of being single, married, having a baby, toddler, school-aged child, and teenagers, then kids leaving home, and retirement. Each season requires a different approach to how we are going to continue working toward our dreams. When we know this and can honor the season of life we are in, we can become empowered to have everything we want at the right time and in the right way. To help us be able to rock your priorities and goals in any season of life, we need to have seasons with F.I.R.E.

Seasons with F.I.R.E. are:

Flexible

Inspired Actions

Relationships

Expectations

Let's dive into how Seasons with F.I.R.E. work.

F – Flexible

The first step to honoring your season of life is finding creative solutions that work within the season of life you are in. The challenge with finding a solution that will work within the season of life you are in is that to find that solution. You are going to need to be very creative.

The other challenge is that even when you find that solution, the season might shift a little in a couple of months, and then you are right back to find a different creative solution again. So how do you get creative to find a solution that will work within your season of life?

Well, first, you need to honestly look at the blessings and challenges of the season of life you are in. In every season of life, there are blessings and challenges; if we understand them, we can use them to our advantage.

When my daughter Arya was a baby, I wanted to work out, but she would often cry when I put her down. So, I started doing a workout program holding her and making it fun for her. I would squat and kiss her when I stood up for the squat. I found a way to work out in the season of life I was in.

I – Inspired Action

The second step in honoring your season of life is to take the actions needed to get it done.

We can be as creative as we want, but if we don't take action on our plan, we will never find a true solution or be effective. We need to be committed to getting it done no matter what. We need to be flexible so we can roll with the punches of life when they come a-swinging.

To make sure we do this, we need a motivator attached to our goals. In the goals section of this book, I go into detail about how to do this, so review that section if you need a reminder. For now, just know if we are going to take action on something, we need to light a fire under our butts; otherwise, we won't start moving.

A motivator helps us to work through the times when our motivation is lacking or when the whirlwinds of life have picked us up and thrown us against the wall. These motivators will help us keep moving forward no matter what season of life we are in.

Years ago, I was trying to learn how to make sales calls, but I was terrified of someone saying no after I pitched them. It took me a while to get my courage up to grab the phone. I would just stare at it, hoping that if I looked at it long enough, I wouldn't actually need to pick it up.

When I finally did pick up the phone, it felt like it weighed a ton. I wasted several hours playing this game, thinking I was doing something when, in reality, I was just thinking about doing something. That pattern drastically changed when there was a motivator put in place.

My boss said that if we didn't reach a certain number of sales in the week, we would not get paid our full pay. This was an effective motivator for me, as I am really attached to feeding my kids. So, I put on my big girl underpants and picked up the phone.

I was in the season of life when I had one child, and she was at preschool for two hours every second day. That was my window of opportunity to work. The moment I dropped her off from school, I would run home and pick up the phone. Then I would be on the phone until I could leave and head out to pick her up, squealing into the parking lot of her school.

Other moms talked about how they worked out together or went for coffee during that 2-hour break. I was working toward my dream of building my own company and regretted nothing.

I was grateful for those hours I had to build my business, and when I picked up my daughter, I took off my boss hat and put on my mommy hat. I did all I could to be present with her.

R - Relationships

Our priorities will usually stay consistent during our seasons of life, but how we approach them will vary widely.

Depending on the season of life we are in, we will have more or less time for each of our priorities. But when we understand F.I.R.E. Priorities, we know that to hit our priorities doesn't need to take a long time, and we can find a way to align with them no matter what season of life we are in.

After I had my daughter Arya, I had two kids under 18 months old. I didn't have the money to hire a babysitter every week, so Andy and I could go on a date, but we still wanted to spend quality time together. One of the ways we did that was to create a make-shift hot tub in our backyard. We attached a hose to our kitchen sink and filled our waist-high kiddie pool with warm water. We would sit out there under the stars listening to music in the magic of the kiddie pool hot tub.

E - Expectations

The last step in honoring your season of life is knowing the season of life you are in.

I am a Canadian, and so I know the harsh reality of seasons. I am very familiar with the dead of winter when my eyelashes would freeze when I went for a run.

I know that in those seasons, when everything felt harsher and like it never would end, it always did. Soon the ice melted, and spring flowers appeared. For us to be able to embrace the season we are in, we need to know that no matter how difficult things are or how crazy life feels, things will change. That season of life will end, and another one will begin. The trick is recognizing the season of life you are in.

We need to manage our expectations, so they fit with the reality of the season of life we are in. For example, a mom with a brand-new baby is going to approach building her business much differently than a mom with teenagers. The brand-new mom needs to set realistic expectations about how she can build her business in between feeding baby and conquering laundry mountain.

Part of managing your expectations is being patient with your progress and forgiving yourself when you make mistakes. The process of embracing the season of life you are in is not an easy one. Things don't usually go as quickly as you would like, life throws many curve balls and sometimes… or if you are like me, often… you mess up. Just know that it is part of the process.

You are supposed to mess up; that is how we learn. The patience required to do great things in life builds the character we need to achieve it.

Digging Deep

Is it possible that you are at a turning point in your life? I believe that because you are reading this, you likely are.

I am going to invite you to ponder a life-changing question of your own. What three things are you not willing to live without? At the end of your life, if you look back and see that you have built your life around these three things, you will know you have lived it well. Write them down because these are the things you need to fight to live your full purpose.

If you would like more support around overcoming the balance myth so that you can have real harmony in your life, go to www.myfirewithin.com/resources to grab your free spot in the My Fire Within Training.

CHAPTER 10:
GOALS WITH FIRE

"It takes as much energy to wish as It does to plan." ~Eleanor Roosevelt

HAVE YOU EVER WONDERED why we set goals on January 1st, and then, within about a month, we have forgotten those ambitions?

I'm sure we can all relate to having things we want to accomplish in life but never do because we either never get started or stop working on them when we hit walls and roadblocks. It is not that we are lazy or bad people; it is just human nature to focus on what is in front of us and do what is the least painful. The challenge is that oftentimes, what is the easiest or least painful is typically what keeps us from growing and accomplishing great things. Giving in to our comfort keeps us stuck in self-doubt, procrastination, and leads to giving up.

One of the biggest challenges Women With Fire faces is that we have big dreams, and we feel like we need to accomplish everything right now! It's okay to feel like we need to take huge leaps toward our goals.

The challenge with doing this is that it is often too big of a leap to start out with, and when we hit a wall or roadblock, we don't have the strength to continue. Let's face it, ladies, when we set a goal, everything gets in the way.

The kids get sick, you get sick, there are bills to pay and clients who need your attention. You are constantly being pulled in a million different directions. It's okay; it's actually part of the process of being a Woman with Fire. Part of the deal to not give up on your dreams is that you have to do a bit of juggling.

That idea of juggling may strike fear into the hearts of some, but no worries, I've got you. I just so happen to have an ace up my sleeve in the form of a little-known secret that will allow you to achieve greatness, starting with just 15 minutes a day. This little bit of magic is what allowed me to write this book beginning with 15 minutes a day, while I was home with a baby and a toddler.

So how then do we push past the times when it gets tough? How do we keep momentum even through the chaos of real life? We can do a couple of things to help us get clear with our goals and stay in momentum, so we can predictably achieve what we want most. I have found this goal-setting system works in every context of life. I have used it in my business to increase profits, write this book, and take my relationships to new heights.

To understand how this goal-setting system works, let me begin with a story. I initially had inspiration come to me that I should write this book but found it difficult to get started and stay in the momentum. I would do great for a couple of days, and then life would get in the way. I would have the same old excuses (not enough time, energy, knowledge…the list could go on and on), and I would stop.

This quote sums it up for me: "The awesome thing about a motivator is that they help keep us focused on our desires rather than our short-term pleasures."

My progress was so slow that I remember thinking that the book might be finished just before my 95th birthday!

Then I created the F.I.R.E. goals system and finally understood how I could set myself up to win. Using this 4-step process, I decided that a reward for hitting my targets would be that I could have a shower after I wrote for 15 minutes.

One night, it was about 10:30 pm, and my husband found me frantically writing in my book. He knew that I would not typically be writing that late, so he said, "Whatcha doing?"

I told him, "I am writing in my book because I really want a shower!"

As you can imagine, this was highly motivating, and I got my book writing session done!

Even though F.I.R.E. goals worked most of the time, I wasn't perfect at it.

Another time, I didn't write in my book and so couldn't have a shower, but I really needed to quickly run into Costco. So, I threw my hair up in a ponytail, put on some clothes, and ran out the door.

While I was at the grocery store, I saw someone that I knew. At that moment, a mental checklist raced through my mind…*did I remember to put on deodorant? Is my shirt clean? I think I have baby spit on me. Did I even comb my hair today?*

Let me tell you, my friend, it only takes a couple of times of running into people you know while tallying up the stinky clothes mental checklist before you are willing to meet any goal so you can get a shower!

After that, I recommitted to my F.I.R.E. goals and, using them, finally wrote the book.

That is the power of this principle. When we know how to take constant, consistent steps toward our goal and how to motivate ourselves even when it is hard, we can achieve any objective. Since then, I have used various motivators to help me get tasks done, such as not being able to go on social media or check my phone until I followed through on my daily goal.

So, what are F.I.R.E. goals? Before we dive into the specifics, we need to understand what gets in the way of us reaching our goals. The first challenge we run into when we are setting goals is that we create broad statements of what we want to accomplish. We rarely get focused, so it is exceptionally difficult to know if we have achieved our goal or not.

We aren't always clear on how we're actually going to achieve the goal, and we don't have a plan for when the chaos of life takes us off track. This is what F.I.R.E. goals are for; to help us get and stay focused and get creative about how we're going to accomplish our goal as we create a sense of urgency that gets the job done.

Many people talk about setting S.M.A.R.T. goals, that is to say, goals that are specific, measurable, attainable, realistic, and have a set time. Although I believe it is wise to be smart about setting goals, I think it is even more critical to have a system that is grounded with a sense of urgency and effective action.

As I have talked about throughout this book, I believe that our goals are lit up when we start with fire. To create a purposeful, prosperous, and passionate life, we will require the fire necessary to take the small, consistent steps toward our dreams and goals even when we can't see the end from the beginning.

F.I.R.E. Goals

Focus & Faith- Focus on one specific goal & have faith you can achieve it and that the Creator will help you.

Incentive - What reward will you get if you do it? What consequence will you get if you don't do it?

Responsible – Are you doing what you said you would?

Exact Time - Use time blocks to work toward your goal

Now let's look at how F.I.R.E. goals get put into practice.

Let's say I want to write a book. I would set a focused goal like, "I will write one chapter of my book every week." I would manage my state of mind, so I have faith that I can accomplish the goal, and I would lean on my Creator for help.

Then I would establish an incentive that would encourage me to accomplish the goal, "I can pick up my phone after I write in my book for 15 minutes a day." I would ensure I am responsible for my goals by telling my husband when I don't write in my book. I would then set an exact time to work toward my goal daily, "I will write in my book for 15 minutes at 7 am every weekday."

This time frame has a set start and end time, and I stay completely focused while I am working on my goal during that time.

Most people who set goals don't use incentives, and so it is easy to quit when going after the goal gets tough. Having F.I.R.E. goals is your secret ingredient to be a Woman with Fire because it will help you move past the walls you hit and will drive you forward to achieve any goal!

I promise that when you apply these principles in your life, you will be able to accomplish the things that are most important to you, stay in momentum with you goals, receive the help you need from the Creator and those around you, find even more peace of mind as you create your dreams in the chaos of life.

Digging Deep

What is one change you want to make in your life?

What is one focused goal that you can do daily that would take you closer to that change?

What is an incentive that you will get when you complete your daily focused goal?

How can you ensure you are responsible for your goal?

What is the exact time you are going to start and end working on this goal?

We know that frequency and ongoing support are critical for lasting change to occur, so I've got another gift to help you.

To claim your free discovery call with a Fire Within Coach, go to www.myfirewithin.com/resources.

SECTION 2:
LIGHT YOUR PROSPERITY

CHAPTER 11:
SECRET #4 PROSPERITY WITH FIRE

"Money can't buy happiness, but it certainly is a stress reliever." ~Besa
Kosava

BEFORE I DIVE INTO TALKING ABOUT creating even more profit, I
need to point out the challenges around money that hold us back.

The first is that we all have baggage around money. It is such an
emotionally charged topic. Although many people say that money doesn't
matter, I love the Zig Ziglar quote that addresses this, "Money isn't the most
important thing in life, but it's reasonably close to oxygen on the 'gotta have
it' scale."

The reality is that we all need money. We need money to live, to
create memories with the people we love, and to help people. The challenge
most entrepreneurs face is that we are often on a wild money roller coaster
ride. We eat last as we work tirelessly to build our business in the hopes of a
better future.

There are times when more money comes in than we thought possible
and times when we are not sure how we are going to keep the lights on in our
house.

Sometimes this wild ride can lead us to feel like a failure during lean
times. We need to understand that all people who have done something great
have sacrificed their short-term comfort for their long-term comfort. Every
successful person I have talked to living their purpose has, at some point,
faced challenges around money.

It is part of the journey, and I believe part of what we need to go
through to be prepared to receive the abundance we are capable of. Going
through lean times helps refine us, encourages us to be resilient, get creative,
and be a good steward of money. It helps us be grateful for what we have and
helps us to be more generous with people in need.

I also need to point out that to create the abundance we want; we
often need to be aware of the beliefs we have around money and change them
for healthier beliefs that will set us free financially. To do this, you can apply
the lessons from the beginning of this book around changing your beliefs and
aligning with the Four Primary Laws of Fire so you can stay in the right

mindset to create the financial success you want. You also will need to fill your mind with new beliefs.

The principles I will cover in the coming pages will help you to ride the money roller coaster less often, will help protect you from the ups and downs of entrepreneurial life, and will help you feel more in control of your money.

Closing the Wealth Gap

Have you ever been excited to get a raise, then used up all the extra money without knowing where it went? There is a principle in play here that keeps the middle-class stuck living paycheck to paycheck while the rich get richer.

If we don't understand this, we will never be able to get ahead, no matter how much money comes in.

I know I have done this. I vividly remember when my husband started making more money than we were expecting each month. We had been struggling financially, and I was desperate for things to change. When I saw the amount of money that was going to be deposited in our account, I was ecstatic!

I wanted to be able to have money to save for an emergency and to pay off the bills that were piling up. Then things just kept coming up that required us to use up the money. Our car broke down; we needed to get more groceries because we were skimping the last couple of months, and things needed to be restocked. We took a trip even though we couldn't really afford it. Without even realizing it, we had spent all of the extra money with nothing to show for it. We do this because we are unaware of a principle that the wealthy know that the poor and middle class do not. This principle is called the Wealth Gap.

When the middle class makes more money, they just increase their expenses and spend any extra money on trips, new cars, a boat, etc. When the rich make more money, they invest the money into a rental property or building up their business. Then they use the cash flow or money they receive from their rental properties and businesses to pay for the things they want like new cars, trips, and a new house. They also manage their money effectively, so they are not spending all of the money they make. They make their money work for them, instead of working for their money, and in the process, they get richer and richer.

This is what the Wealth Gap looks like:

When I learned about this principle, I realized that I was stuck on the wrong side of the Wealth Gap. It is a basic human phenomenon that we spend the amount of money we have. I am definitely guilty of this. I knew that if I was going to change this pattern in myself, I would need to find a solution that made it easy for me to save and harder for me to spend everything.

I am incredibly grateful for the Fire Principles I have learned about creating financial security so I can close the money gap. To apply these principles to a metaphor, I am going to share with you how to grow your very own money tree.

Growing Your Money Tree

Most of us are seeking financial freedom. We want money to do what we want and to have enough money not only to buy the things we need but the things we want. I get it.

Believe me; I get it. I want that too! However, I think often in our chase for financial freedom; we miss the mark of achieving financial security first.

We need to understand certain principles to have the financial freedom to weather the storms of life. The storms that inevitably come to us all; the loss of a job, the loss of a loved one, economic downturns, illness, or injuries. These things happen unexpectedly, and when they do, we don't have time to build financial security; we need it to be there already to catch us.

So, what do we need to do to create financial security in our lives you may be asking? I am going to share with you the principles that I know to be true. In this world of confusing financial advice with several experts arguing against one another, a few simple principles cut through all the noise. They are so simple and easy that almost no one is doing them.

They likely will be things you have heard before, so you may be tempted to brush them off because you "already know them." If you have this feeling, I encourage you to think again and ask yourself if you are DOING them. Are you applying them in your own life? Is there more you could do to apply them?

In the spirit of transparency, I want you to know that I am striving to achieve these principles, too. I didn't grow up knowing them, I have made every financial mistake known to man and likely ones other people didn't even think of! I am on a journey of healing my own financial security. I tell you that, so you know you are not alone on this journey and that no matter where you are, it is okay to start right from there.

Before we begin, I am going to warn you that these financial principles may not be easy to hear. I know when I first heard them, I felt a little overwhelmed and unsure if I could follow them. I know now that it is possible to follow them if we just take it one step of faith and patience at a time. I also know that not only are these principles true, but they will protect us from stress, worry, and financial ruin. I know that because I have been on the edge of that financial uncertainty myself.

I am grateful for the abundance I have experienced in my life as well as the harder times because it has taught me how important it is to create financial security for my family. It showed me how uncertain and stressful life is without a financial security plan.

I understand that this plan needs to be not an "I will get to it one-day" plan, it needs to be an "I will do what it takes to create financial security for my family" kind of plan. I never want to be in such a dangerous financial situation again, and I am grateful for these principles that will help me ensure we are protected. I want your family to be protected, too. This is why I am sharing them with you.

I have seen some of these principles discussed in many different ways. Many of these financial principles have been inspired by the Church of Jesus Christ of Latter-Day Saints[7,] but I have also heard parts of them echoed in other churches, with Dave Ramsey, and even though Tony Robbins.

The thing I love most about truth is that it appears in many different contexts. The truth I am going to share with you gathers all of the true financial principles and puts them in one easy to understand place.

It Starts with a Seed

To begin growing a tree...even a money tree, we need to begin with a seed.

It is the beginning of what is possible. It is the tiny seed that appears so insignificant, but in reality, it is what will shift everything. In this example, the seed is first to have faith.

It first requires faith in the Creator. Faith that the Creator wants you to succeed and will help you along the way. You also need to have faith in yourself. Faith that you are capable of achieving success. You need to know in your core that even when you fall down, you will get back up and that in the end, you will find a way to create the financial security you want.

You also need to have faith in your partner and be unified in your desire to grow your money tree. When you are both committed to creating financial security, you will be able to work together to create it. This is critical so that one of you is not undoing your financial progress along the way. After all, if one of you is focused on saving, and your partner is focused on spending, you won't get very far.

Being unified means working together to solve the situation together in a spirit of love and compassion instead of a spirit of blame, contention, or making unilateral decisions.

Grow Roots

The next part of your financial security is growing roots.

Two kinds of roots are most important to growth. One is to help you build your wealth; the other is to help you save your wealth. They work together and support one another. The first root builds your wealth through work. It is a divine principle that in this life, we need to work. It not only helps us provide for the necessities of life for ourselves and our family, but it increases our feelings of self-worth and our capacity.

In this case, I am talking about work that brings in income. The bottom line is that if you need more money to create the financial security you need; you need to make more money. If you want to make more money, you need to do what it takes to bring in more income.

The second root is being able to budget effectively. I know that sounds basic, but I am surprised to know that, according to a study by U.S. Bank, 41 percent of Americans say they use a budget.[8] That means that most people are not using a budget.

This is a serious issue because if we don't know where our money is going, we can't make decisions about where we want it to go. I used to do something called "black hole budgeting." I had no idea how much money I had when people took it out, and when it was deposited into my account. I would stand in the checkout line with pangs of anxiety as they ran my bank card through the machine.

Budgeting, although it is not always easy, is critical, so we know where we are really at and can make decisions about where we want to go and a plan to do it.

There are a lot of free resources online, so find a budgeting plan that works for you. It doesn't need to be fancy; it just needs to work. Now, of course, the most important part of having a budget is following it! That's why I will walk you through a money plan called Prosperity Accounts that helps you to stick to your budget in a way that is easy and accounts for real-life... It doesn't involve carrying envelopes around with you or if you are like me, leaving them at home and falling off the budget wagon!

Setting up prosperity accounts was game-changing for me because I could focus on saving for our future instead of spending all the extra money that came in. It also made it easy for me to follow, so I no longer felt guilty spending money because I had already set aside what we needed!

To get prosperity accounts set up, I just went to a bank that didn't charge service fees for having multiple accounts. I opened enough bank accounts to cover all the different areas of life that we spent money on and made sure that there were no overdrafts. I set up separate bank accounts for things like income, bills, family spending, my spending, Andy's spending, emergency, charity, taxes, health savings, kids recreation, vacations, and maintenance. Then I arranged for my income to be deposited into my "income account" and set up weekly automated transfers to the various other accounts.

When we started this process, the amounts were small because we did not have a lot of money at the time. Some of our accounts just had $1 transferred to them every week. It doesn't really matter how much money you put in the different accounts; it is just important to start with whatever you have.

I got a bank card for the main account that I would spend money from, and when I bought something, I would just transfer money to that account and use my debit card to buy it.

This allowed me to know with certainty that money would be in the accounts when I needed it. It also made it easier for me to save and helped me to clearly follow my budget because everything was automatic.

The Tree Trunk
To grow the trunk of our money tree, we need first to give (some people call this tithing).

I know it seems contrary to human logic to give money away, especially when you are struggling financially. I can definitely relate to this feeling. When I first learned about the Fire Principle of giving and that I needed to give 10 percent of my money to charity or a church, I panicked, as I shared with you earlier in the book.

I understand that aligning with the law of giving doesn't always result in financial blessings. Sometimes our burdens are emotionally lifted, or we are uplifted and strengthened in other ways. I learned from that experience though that inspiration and blessings come after the trial of our faith and that as we take action to do what is right, even when we don't know how it will all work out, we receive more than we can imagine.

The Bark

Next, we need bark for our money tree.

The bark is critical to protect you from the financial storms of life. If you don't have savings, start with the goal of putting aside $1000 for emergencies. This allows you to have a cushion for when emergencies happen, so you don't need to rely on debt for these unexpected circumstances. It needs to be said here, though, that your emergency fund can only be used for emergencies.

Keep it in a place that is accessible but not so accessible that you will be tempted to dip into it to pay for things that aren't emergencies. Also, make sure that you replace your emergency fund as soon as possible when you use some of it.

It may not be easy to come up with the $1000 but start with what you have and commit to doing what it takes to reach that amount. Go back to the walls of your financial security house. Work more to create more income or reduce your spending so you can save more of what you have.

After you have built up your $1000 emergency fund, commit to keep building! Work toward an emergency fund that covers your expenses for a month. When you get that taken care of, work toward saving for 3-6 months of expenses (after you have handled your debt).

Another aspect of the bark of our money tree is having insurance to protect your family during difficult times by securing adequate life, disability, health, and home insurance. I learned how important having insurance is when my daughter Zoe contracted a life-threatening illness and needed to be flown to a hospital. Our hospital bills were around $60,000, and without insurance, that would have been a huge financial burden for our family at a time when we needed to be focusing on our daughter's health, not financial worries.

The Branches

For us to be able to branch out and achieve our dreams, the debt can't stop our growth.

Staying out of consumer debt or working toward getting out of debt are the branches of our money tree. I know we live in a society where we feel like we need to have a big house, new car, fancy clothes, and to go on vacations often. However, these things really are wants, not needs. Is it okay to enjoy the luxuries of life? Absolutely!

We just need to make sure we are not enjoying these things by going into debt. I have learned this lesson the hard way. I have taken many trips riding the coattails of debt only to feel anxiety and then come home to a mountain of debt. I have also spent over $46,000 just to hold debt. This was an eye-opening experience for me.

Ralf Waldo Emerson said that "A man (or woman) in debt is so far a slave." All I know is that when I have debt, I feel stressed, and it is very hard to get out of it.

If you're in debt, I don't want you to feel bad. That is not my intention. I just want you to know that there is another way to live that doesn't involve the stress that comes with debt. Make a commitment to take steps toward becoming debt-free so you can keep the money that comes your way instead of owing it to creditors. You don't need to tackle your debt all at once; you just need to pay what you can and seek to find ways to pay off more debt through making more money and budgeting more effectively.

As Dave Ramsey recommends, pay off one debt at a time.[9] Start with the debt with the least amount owing or with the largest interest rate. As you pay off one debt, take the money you spent on that debt and put it toward the next one. As you continue to do this, your ability to pay off debt will increase with momentum. People often refer to this as a debt rollover program.

You may need to go into debt for a few expenses in life. These include a modest home (some recommend keeping your mortgage to be less than 25 percent of your income), a modest car, and schooling that will help you make more money. The rules for personal debt and business debt are different, as well. In business, you can use debt when you have confidence that it will create a return on your investment quickly.

The Leaves

Now that our money tree is growing, we can grow leaves. The leaves are the money we use to invest in the future. Some of the ways we invest money are through business and real estate. To be successful in any of these areas, we need to have a few elements in place.

First, we need a success mindset. This is critical because to create the results we want on the outside, we need to begin by creating the results we want on the inside. That is why I have spent so much time on this book. I hope it helps you develop the mindset you need to create the life you want. Without this mindset, we are stopped before we even begin.

Next, we need the knowledge required to achieve the financial results we want. Having proximity to someone who has already done what we want to do is critical because it gives us a guide who knows how to help us to overcome the biggest challenges regarding our money so we can avoid making their mistakes. It saves us time, saves us money, and speeds up our success.

Now we are ready to start a business. Business is wonderful because it has a lot of potential to make a high profit. However, it can be unpredictable as the market shifts, and it takes time, resources, and energy to build a successful business.

That is why I love the health company that I partnered with because it allows people who want to create residual income do so with little to no risk. All the marketing, resources, distribution, and training are provided, and business owners just plug into the system and share the health products they love. All the while, they are building residual income, being part of an incredible community of people committed to service and getting in the best shape of their life.

Business and real estate are so powerful because you can use money from your business to buy real estate and the real estate can help you hold your money to hedge against the ups and downs of business.

I used to feel like going into real estate was too risky. Then my mentor helped me understand that the rich invest in real estate. They invest in it because they know this little-known secret that real estate is a predictable investment that increases in value and is insurable. It's insurable because when your house burns down, your insurance gives you money to build a new one. They also know that when they use a strategy of keeping their property long-term and predictably renting out their properties, they can use the cash flow they receive from their rental property to pay for their lifestyle.

Why not have someone else pay your mortgage and give you money to travel.

The Fruit

Now that you have built financial success, we can use the fruit of your labor to commit to helping people in need. Share the wealth that you have built with people who need your help. Money is really a resource that helps us to create the life we want, and we have a responsibility to share that wealth to help others.

Part of sharing the wealth with our kids is teaching them these principles of financial abundance and responsibility. We need to teach them money facts, so eventually, they will grow their own money tree.

Grow Your Money Tree

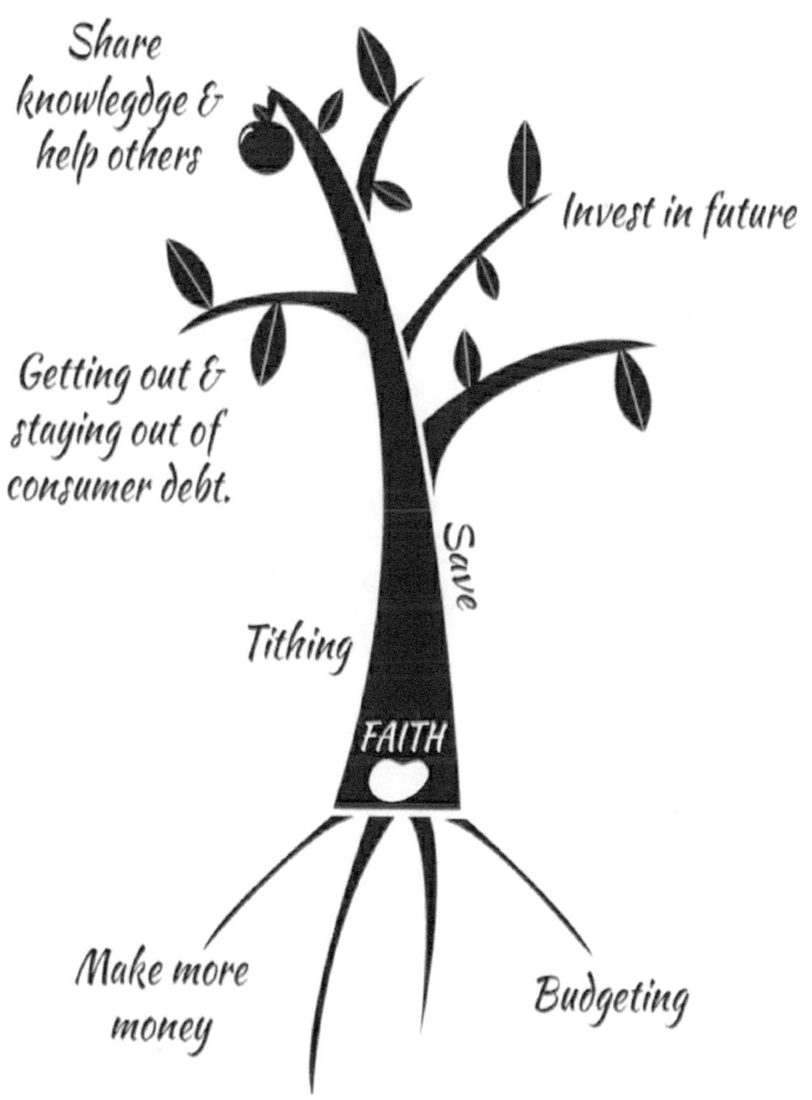

My Money Wake Up Call

I thought we were completely secure.

I was an international speaker and coach, and so was my husband.

Andy was working full-time with a company we believed in, and I was staying home with our kids and working part-time as a coach. We had a steady income and thought we were fairly financially secure.

Then the company Andy was working for changed directions, and his position was no longer relevant. It happened that I was tied to the same company and so my coaching business dried up. Within one month, we had no paycheck. We were not able to get a traditional job because we were in another country on a work visa, and we did not have savings.

We feared we would lose our home because we didn't have enough to pay for our mortgage. We had barely enough money to buy groceries, and I was feeling so stressed that my hair was falling out.

I have never before been at a point in my life when I needed help financially, but this time, we desperately needed help. Our church helped us cover some of our expenses. Although I was incredibly grateful, I was also ashamed and felt tremendous guilt.

We decided that we would do whatever it took to never be in that position again. We were determined to build our business so we could build residual income to protect our family from the financial storms of life and committed to supporting others to protect their families financially by supporting them in building their businesses.

I am so grateful for these financial principles that have helped me to build residual income, create $20,000 in a day through a real estate investment, and give us the peace of mind to be able to financially protect our family.

Life is Short…Live Your Purpose

We have to love our work because life is short.

I have talked to many people who start or join businesses that they half-heartedly care about. This just will not work, or if it does work, you will not be as happy as you could be. Every single person in this world has this light inside them. You have it too! It is that one thing that you love more than anything. That thing that you could talk all day about. The one that when you are doing it, you lose track of time and work doesn't feel like work at all. Sometimes it feels a little like play. If you can make a business doing work you love, you are going to live your purpose, and work won't feel much like work at all.

In fact, research shows that "having identified a purpose in life (is) associated with greater life satisfaction…"[10] This validates the idea that when we are living our purpose and have hope that we are capable of living our potential, we are happier in our life. You are going to be able to push through the times when work or your business feels tough, and you hit walls, and you feel like giving up. You are going to be able to push past it all because that fire within you is lit, and you love what you do.

If you cannot find a way to live your passion for doing work you love, at least find a way to do it in your personal time. Life is too short! Do what you love!

I know without a doubt that all people are given gifts from the Creator. Oftentimes, you can have talents that come naturally to you that you might not think are a big deal. The challenge with things that come naturally to us is that we don't realize that they don't come naturally to everyone else.

We tend to underestimate the importance of them and see them as not a big deal. The truth is that they are a very big deal. We are all given unique gifts and talents from the Creator. We need to understand that we are given these gifts to share with others to improve their lives and help us grow.

Do Work That Makes a Difference

One of the biggest challenges I see women entrepreneurs make in their work is that either they do work they love and don't have a vehicle to make money from it, or they do work they don't love.

The challenge with doing work you love but not having a vehicle to make money from it is that it is not sustainable. You want to serve, which is completely awesome, but you also need to feed your family. At the end of the day, you will spend most of your time on things that feed your family. When you do work, you don't love; you are not stepping into your purpose. You have a unique purpose, and when you are not stepping into it by using your talents and fueling your passion, your life will feel like it is missing something because it is.

When you can find work that you love, that actually serves people, and that has a vehicle attached to it so you can make money, you are set up to win and to help others win alongside with you. The really amazing thing is that when you align your purpose and passion with a business vehicle, you will be able to serve in a more powerful way than you can imagine, you will be more effective in your work, and you will feel happier.

When My Business Made No Money

I started a business years ago interviewing successful business owners.

The idea was that I would have a website where people could go to listen to the interviews, and I would have affiliate links on the website to make money from services advertised. However, it was not planned out at all. I didn't know how to get people from listening to the interviews to clicking on the affiliate links. I loved interviewing people, but I was making no money.

I realized that I needed to find a way to connect my work to a vehicle that would create revenue. Years later, I created the My Fire Within Radio podcast. I wanted to interview successful women and share their real and raw stories of juggling work, family, and everything in between.

However, I didn't want to fall into the same trap of doing something I love without having a vehicle attached to it. This is why I decided to partner with a health company that fits my mission, and that truly helps women with weight management, energy, sleep, and to feel less stressed. I could share it as an affiliate so I could have another income stream to my business simply by sharing the health system that changed my life.

Since then, I have partnered with several successful and famous coaches, models, and best-selling authors so they can also be an affiliate to create another smart income stream for their own brands.

Digging Deep

I promise you have something within you already, that can make your life and the lives of others better.

Do you know what it is?

Are you using it to your full capacity?

The thing about talents is that they need to be developed. We start with a desire to do something or a natural talent, but it is only when we put in work and time and effort to develop it when we really can shine. Are you putting in the time to develop your talents? How could you use your talents even more to help the people around you?

I know that as you use your talents, you will be lifted, strengthened, and feel more joy in this life. After all, if we don't use it, we lose it. So, use it! Step out and be willing to be your best self. Even when you're scared, and you worry what others will think about you, and you worry that you are not enough. You are enough. You were made for this. Everything you need is already within you.

If would like support and to know how you can align your business

with even more purpose, book a free discovery call with a Fire Within Coach here:
www.myfirewithin.com/resources.

SECTION 3:
LIGHT YOUR PASSION

CHAPTER 12:
SECRET #5 RELATIONSHIPS WITH FIRE

"Love doesn't just sit there, like a stone. It has to be made, like bread; remade all the time, made new." ~Ursula K. Le Guin

Relationships Are Everything

IF YOU THINK THAT THE STRUGGLES you are facing in your relationship don't influence your ability to make money, your happiness, and your health, then you are dead wrong.

As Dr. Sue Johnson points out in her book, *Hold Me Tight,* "The Heart Attack & Stroke Center for Cognitive and Social Neuroscience at the University of Chicago, calculates that loneliness raises blood pressure to the point where the risk of heart attack and stroke is doubled."[11] Sociologist James House of the University of Michigan declares that "...emotional isolation is a more dangerous health risk than smoking or high blood pressure, and we now warn everyone about these two!"[12]

So, what does that tell us about the importance of having connected relationships? If we don't have happy, healthy relationships, it will literally kill us. After all, how can we possibly create a life with awesome businesses! A purposeful and passionate life; when we will die early of a heart attack or stroke?

Having a great relationship doesn't just protect us from experiencing difficult health conditions; it lowers our stress, increases our mental health, and even our ability to deal with physical and emotional pain. Having a connected relationship is the single most important thing we can do to be happier, less stressed out, more effective in our work, and to be healthier.

There was a point when I went to Brandon, desperate to change our financial situation. "We need to make more money," I told him. We had tried everything to make more money. We had tried investing in stocks, joined an MLM, started our own business, but we were just losing money, time, sanity, and our connection with each other.

Then Brandon asked a question that pierced me to the soul and helped me begin to understand that I needed to clean things up in my relationship to clean things up on my bank statement. He asked, "How is your relationship?" *My relationship?* I thought, *why on earth is he asking about my relationship?*

I was a little offended as I blurted out, "It's fine!"

It wasn't fine, though. At the time, we were working day and night. I was frustrated and resentful of Andy, and he was feeling ignored and rejected. He was turning to pornography to meet his physical needs, and I had convinced myself that I didn't really need sex, so I was opting for a life of abstinence. Our relationship was a mess, and the awesome marriage that we once had was nowhere to be seen.

Brandon could hear the frustration in my voice, and he began to explain how the health of my relationship with my husband would directly impact our ability to make more money. It was at that moment that I realized that if I truly wanted to live an abundant life, I needed to be willing to go into the messy areas and clean them up.

I needed to be willing to do the work required to create an awesome marriage. After all, what is the point of having a lot of money with no one to share it with?

I committed to following Brandon's advice on how to create a passionate marriage, and so Andy and I began to use the Fire Principles to save our marriage. It was not easy at first. It took some letting go of hurt feelings and resentments and some opening of our eyes to really seeing each other and being willing to use the skills to get closer together even when we didn't want to.

In the end, though, it was so worth it! I can honestly say that our marriage is better today than the day we got married. My husband has become my hero, and he looks at me like a goddess. I love our life together, and I can see now that as we have improved our marriage, we were able to improve our profits. We were able to replace our incomes from our jobs and have enough income to move to the house of our dreams and see the world.

I love that these principles help people who already are in a relationship to make it even better and that they also help people who are single to prepare themselves to create an incredible relationship in the future. So how do we create a connected relationship, so we can experience even more of the prosperity and passion we want? It starts with the bond.

It's All About the Bond

The bond is basically when we feel close and connected with the people we love the most. It is that feeling like they have your back. It is what we need in relationships to feel truly loved and supported by our partner. As Dr. Sue

Johnson says, "Our connection with the people we love is the foundation of our happiness, sense of security, and love in this. world."

The following section about the bond is my view of this subject that was also addressed by Dr. Sue Johnson's incredible work in her book *Love Sense*.[13]

When we are not bonded, we feel disconnected from our partners and feel like they don't have our back. We say something, or our partner says something that hurts us, creating a bond injury—and we go into panic mode.

Research shows that the same part of our brain is activated when we are not bonded as when we are in physical pain. In her book *Hold Me Tight: Seven Conversations for a Lifetime of Love*, Dr. Sue Johnson says that "When love doesn't work, we hurt." Indeed, "hurt feelings" is a precisely accurate phrase, according to psychologist Naomi Eisenberger of the University of California. Her brain imaging studies show that rejection and exclusion trigger the same circuits in the same part of the brain, the anterior cingulate, as physical pain.[14]

When we have conflict in our relationship, there are three ways that we tend to respond. We either become anxious trying to get reassurance that our partner supports us, we become avoidant trying to avoid the conflict altogether, or we resolve the conflict in a loving way and stay bonded.

We have developed these patterns as children as a response to our parents. The patterns are not good or bad; they have helped us get through life to this point. In all the patterns of dealing with a bond injury, we are always just trying to stay safe and know the other person has our back. The patterns can create complications in the relationship, so we need to choose healthier patterns that help us to feel more bonded.

The Bond

Bond Injury

In my relationship with Andy, our pattern of dealing with conflict is that I am anxious, and he is avoidant. There was one time when he was doing the dishes, and I went to talk to him.

Unbeknownst to me, he had only one of his EarPods in his ear and was listing to an audiobook. I didn't see it so I thought he could hear me. I started telling him all the things that were bothering me and opening up about how I felt like I couldn't do it all and asking for reassurance that I was a good mother.

I finished talking, and he said nothing. I got angry and shouted, "I don't need your approval anyway!" He only heard my last loud statement, and not knowing what had just happened and why I was angry with him, pulled his earphone out. His tendency is to avoid the conflict, so he felt the temptation to just put the earphone back in and ignore my seemingly crazy outburst, but because he knows about the bond, he asked me what was going on, and we began to heal the bonding injury to get reconnected.

If that same situation had happened before learning about the bond, we would have spiraled out of control with blaming and anger, both of us not getting our needs met. I'm so grateful, we learned about the bond and knew how to recover when the bonding injury happened. After doing that, we were more connected than before and felt completely loved.

Healing the Bond

It is a simple process to heal when a bond injury has happened. By the way, it is completely natural that we are going to hurt each other's feelings, and that the bond will slip at times. This is part of being in a relationship. The magic comes when you know this is part of the process and how to heal the bond, so you are closer than you were before the injury.

To heal the bond, both people need to have an open heart and the willingness to get reconnected. The person who has been hurt simply follows the Four Steps to Healing the Bond.

Step One: Assume the best - assume the best about your partner and share how you feel in a respectful way.

Step Two: Share your fear - at the core of a bonding injury is the feeling that your partner doesn't have your back. Share with them what you are most afraid of. I.e., "I am afraid you will leave."

Step Three: Ask for what you need. Too often, we expect our partner to know what we want. They are not a mind reader; we have to ask for what we need. I.e., "I need you to tell me you love me."

Step Four: Your partner needs to respond by being attentive, respond to what you are saying, and be willing to give you what you need.

To give you an example of how we used the Four Steps to Healing the Bond in the story I told earlier in this chapter, this is how we used it. I assumed the best by reminding myself that Andy loves me. I was vulnerable and shared my fear by telling him that I was afraid that he didn't think I was good enough. I asked for what I needed by asking for him to tell me I am enough and that he loves me. He responded by listening to what I was saying, letting me know he heard me, telling me he loves me and that I am enough, and giving me a huge hug. This process takes minutes, but the effects of it last a lifetime as we get closer together through these conversations.

When the Four Steps to Healing the Bond are done, it is incredible how much more connected you will feel with the people you love. Since Andy and I have done this, I have felt more loved than ever before, and I feel like we are more of a team.

Four Keys to Unlock Passion
The bond is most important in a relationship. It is what makes everything else work. These Three Keys to Unlock Passion help take the bond to the next level. They help couples to feel connected no matter what is going on in the world around them.

Key #1 - Connecting in the Chaos
In today's society, with so many things occupying our time and pulling us in a million directions, it can be difficult to stay unified with our partner. Between school, work, family, chores, cooking, cleaning, kid's activities, social engagements, and everything involved in running a family and business, we can easily get lost in the day to day of survival. This is risky for a couple because when we are not connected, we can be like ships passing in the night. Living together but not truly connecting.

Love is something we actively create with someone. It takes being bonded, and this takes work. So how do we stay connected with our partner when life is crazy busy? One way is to make sure we know how the other person is feeling and know what we can do to help them feel loved. How often do we go about our day and have no idea what our partner is going through? This is a very dangerous pattern because it can lead to selfishness. When we are too focused on how we are feeling about things and have no awareness about how our partner is feeling, we can think our feelings are more important, and we don't see the needs of our partner.

So how do we connect and know what is going on for the other person? It's simple, really, but it requires consistent effort and a desire to truly connect. You can do this by using a tool called a "check-in." When Andy and I do this with each other, we are able to stay connected throughout the day, no matter what is going on. We know how to support each other, and we both feel more loved. We strive to do this "feeling-check" two times a day.

How to do a feeling-check: take turns asking each other the following questions.

1. How are you feeling, and why? (Then you reflect on what they said, "So you're feeling…?")
2. What can I do to help you feel loved?

Key #2 - Make Life an Adventure

I will never forget the moment when I realized that this one thing would make or break a family, make or break a business, or make or break a life.

It is the one thing that breathes life into a relationship, gives life passion, and creates a constant adventure. To say it is awesome would be an understatement. What am I talking about? I am talking about something called Bright Futures. Bright Futures are plans that you create with yourself, your partner, your family, and your business that you can't wait to experience, and they make life feel like an adventure!

The problem today is that most people think they are too busy for date night, fun family adventures and things to look forward to in their business. Another challenge is that if people do take a break, they make it a huge vacation that they have to wait all year to experience.

They work tirelessly for that one vacation that they get to look forward to, and then once it is over, it is a huge let down as they go back to the grind, so they can earn enough to escape their life again in another year. You don't have to wait for that once a year vacation to love life. Start loving life right now, this week, today.

The key to being able to do this is to set up consistent Bright Futures. To do this effectively, you will need to set up three kinds of Bright Futures. One for this week, one for this next month, and one for the next six months to a year. If you aren't in a relationship, set these Bright Futures for yourself! What things could you do in those time frames that you would love to do? It doesn't need to cost much or anything at all. Get creative!

If you are in a relationship, set these Bright Futures together. One of the most effective ways to do this is to have one person gives their partner three choices of what you can do together. Then the other person picks from that list something they would like to do. The benefit of doing this is that it avoids the dreaded, "I don't know, what do you want to do," cycle, and helps both people find something they would like to do.

To take it to the next level, set Bright Futures in your family and your business. In the family, it creates more of a sense of excitement and working together. In business, it creates more of a team and a willingness to collaborate and work more effectively.

Key #3 - Pure Moments

So often, we feel like we need a full day or a big activity to really connect with someone.

I used to feel like that, and I felt disappointed that my life was not like a romantic movie. I felt like I couldn't have fun and connect with my husband unless we were having a date night.

Then I learned about the power of Pure Moments. I learned that we could connect with people in a moment, and that moment in time is what they will remember. When I realized this, I began looking for Pure Moments I could create with Andy in the midst of our chaotic life.

Key #4 - Fireworks in the Bedroom

The two biggest issues couples fight about are sex and money.

We already know that when a couple is not bonded, it affects our productivity, happiness, stress level, and health. So, why is that we rarely talk about intimacy in a business context? Well, ladies, if we are going to create a passionate life, that is going to include passion in the bedroom. It has to. When we are truly bonded with our partner, intimacy is the thing that will connect us emotionally, spiritually, and physically.

If it is so important, why are so many couples struggling in silence with a disconnect in the bedroom? I think it is because there are not many spaces where we can talk about it openly and in a respectful way. We do have to talk about it, though.

When Andy and I got married, we had an incredible relationship... including inside the bedroom. Then when kids came along, and sleepless nights and financial stress, we found that we were not connecting physically. When we were intimate, I often did it out of obligation. Andy felt unwanted and alone, and I felt resentful and angry. We wanted to connect with each other, but we didn't know how to. I went to books for answers and got insane advice to think about someone else while being intimate.

Then I realized that for things to change, I must change. I started making passion a priority in my life by making space to spend time with Andy that didn't involve a TV. We focused on being bonded throughout the day. We committed to being respectful and present with each other in the bedroom. These things helped us to truly connect with each other emotionally, physically, and spiritually. We fell in love all over again.

As women, we are told so many myths about intimacy. That everything needs to be perfect; we need to look perfect; we need to be skilled lovers. These things are myths. Real intimacy happens in unplanned moments when we are truly bonded with the person we love. It is imperfect and beautiful. We can unleash this part of our lives when we accept our own and our partner's perfect imperfections; we get to know what each other likes and are respectful and in love with one another. Intimacy is a sacred part of a relationship, and it bonds us in a way that nothing else can. Our relationships are worth fighting for, and that includes fighting for passionate intimacy!

If you get a sense that I have a lot more to say about relationships, you would be right. I am so passionate about relationships because I believe they are what this life is really about. I am holding back some of the floodgates on creating incredible and passionate relationships simply because there is not enough room in the pages of this book. I need to open the floodgates onto the pages of an upcoming book, all about *relationships with fire.*

I know that the information I have given you in this book will help you right now in having even more connected, passionate, and loving relationships. I am excited about the future, too, because I would love to give you even more!

Digging Deep

Can you commit to doing daily Feeling Checks with your partner?

What weekly, short-term, and longer-term bright futures can you set with your partner?

How can you create daily pure moments with your partner?

SECTION 4:
LIGHT YOUR HEALTH

CHAPTER 13:
SECRET #6 HEALTH WITH FIRE

"Communities and countries and ultimately, the world, are only as strong as the health of their women." ~Michelle Obama

HOW COULD I POSSIBLY TALK about lighting your fire to create the life you have always wanted without talking about your health?

Let's be super real here. If you do not have your health, you are going to die or be very sick. How can you possibly live your purpose, create awesome relationships, and create abundance financially when you are not on this earth? I know that sounds basic, and yet how many times do we let the chaos of life get in the way of us taking care of our bodies?

We know what we need to do. It is pretty simple, but are we actually doing it? We know we need to get enough sleep, eat lots of fruits and vegetables, exercise every day, and not stress out. And yet how often do we get busy with life and not get enough sleep because we are up all night with our kids, not have time to plan meals, so we find ourselves snacking on the cake when we get hungry at 3:00 in the afternoon. We have all the best intentions in the world for working out, and on January first, we start crushing it. But after about two weeks pass, we get sick or crazy busy with our work, and our workouts fall by the wayside.

The reality is life gets in the way if we let it. The other reality is that when life gets in the way, we have to get back up and try again to create the health we want because if we don't, we will be giving up our future for right now. I am telling you all of this with an understanding of how hard it can be to take care of ourselves.

I am a closet-eating-chocolate-chip-cookie-loving woman when I get stressed out. I have gone months without working out and know the feeling of facing the dreaded swimsuit season with absolute terror. The lesson that I have to take care of myself, so I can create the life I want, came when I found out that I have a health condition that would affect me for the rest of my life.

My journey of having this disease occurred after I had my first baby Zoe when I developed a condition that caused me to gain weight. This was super-fantastic since I'd just had a baby and felt part walrus already. It also caused me to have symptoms of feeling down. I felt anxious, was extremely tired, and my emotions were unpredictable.

I went to the doctor and was given medication for my health issue. My doctor told me to take pills for the rest of my life and that it would be okay. It wasn't okay, though. I didn't know that my diet and lifestyle could make my condition worse and that those little pills I took every day we're helping my symptoms but not curing my illness.

I got worse until I developed a serious health condition that caused several food sensitivities. I couldn't eat gluten, sugar, dairy, or soy. If I ate any of these foods, I got really sick for hours. Sounds fun, right?

When I found out what my condition meant, I cried for a week. I LOVE all things made of wheat, dairy, and sugar, and I couldn't even imagine a life where I wasn't eating the foods that I loved.

I hadn't been able to go without eating chocolate for a month, let alone forever! I knew though that I wanted to be healthy for the long haul, that I needed to be there for my kids and my husband. I didn't want to give up on my future dreams and plans simply out of convenience and deliciousness.

So, I put on my big girl panties and started learning how I could still eat incredible and yummy food that wouldn't make me sick. I learned how to make dairy-free, milk chocolate brownies, cakes, and even chocolate turtles that are so unbelievably delicious.

I will never forget the day I became committed to doing whatever it took to work toward healing my body. I was going on a date with Andy. We had finally found a restaurant where I could eat. I had been waiting all week and could almost taste the food and was full of anticipation as I stood in a line. When it was finally my turn to order, I got up to the cashier and ordered the only thing I could eat on the menu: gluten-free pizza with dairy-free cheese. The cashier told me they were out of dairy-free cheese, and I realized there was nothing I could eat in the restaurant.

We got back into the car, and Andy called several restaurants trying to find something I could eat. But there was nothing. I cried in the car because I was worried this was how my life was going to be forever. I feared that I wouldn't be able to enjoy holiday dinners with my family or date nights.

I am grateful for that moment because it sent me on a quest to figure out what happened to my body and how I could find healing. After doing some research, I realized that for me to heal from this condition, I needed to heal my gut. I learned that so many of the physical and emotional health issues we face could be corrected by healing our gut health.

People had talked to me about gut health for a long time, but I never really understood it. There are lots of incredible books on gut health.

Basically, research shows that the gut is so important that it is considered to be our second brain. In fact, we produce more serotonin (a chemical that is known as the "happy hormone") in our gut than in our brain. There is good microbiota in our gut, and they are helping us to stay healthy and to feel happy. There is always a battle going on within our body between the good microbiota and bad bacteria.

We can strengthen the good microbiota by feeding them fruits and vegetables, drinking enough water, getting exercise, getting enough sleep, and not being stressed out. We feed the bad bacteria through sugar, processed food, not getting enough sleep or exercise, and stress. It is critical for our health that we strengthen the good microbiota so we can win the battle within our body so that we can be healthy and happy. I learned that gut health had been linked to a variety of health conditions ranging from autoimmune disease, skin conditions, depression, anxiety, and even weight loss.

I knew I needed to take steps to improve my gut health and support my body with feeling better. Even though I knew that I needed to do this to be healthy and happy, sometimes life got in the way. I was tired of the diet roller coaster, and I wanted to experience optimal health. One of the things I have found so helpful in eating healthy first thing in the morning is having a healthy protein shake with lots of spinach. It was important to me to find a health system that had the highest standards because I understand that not all health companies are created equal, and some even put sugar in their protein shakes.

I am so grateful that my friend told me about a health system that has helped me turn my health around! Although my health is not perfect, I have had dramatic improvements and can now eat food without getting sick! For me, that is seriously a miracle! I have a lot more energy, my mood is much better, and as a bonus, I even dropped a dress size! My husband Andy has dropped over 55 pounds and found his abs!

When this changed our lives so much, we realized that we needed to share it with others. I began sharing it with people who wanted even more energy, better sleep, who needed to support their gut in healing or wanted weight management. After talking with many women, I discovered something incredible. I would ask them about the health goals they had, and often, they would share that they wanted to lose five, 10, or even 100 pounds.

When we would explore further what was an important goal for them, they would share what it was about much more than the number on the scale. They would disclose how the weight was impacting how they saw themselves and that when they looked in the mirror, the reflection staring back at them did not match who they felt like inside. They would explain that they couldn't connect with their husband intimately because they didn't feel sexy and felt uncomfortable in their own skin.

These women would tell me that they wanted to feel better because they felt like they were not honoring the body their Creator gave to them, and they wanted to have more of the energy they wanted so they could live their purpose. They shared that their health issues were getting in the way of them having enough energy to play with their kids or their grandkids, that they worried about their future, and that they didn't want to become a burden for the people they love.

It was through these stories that I began to understand how important health is to reach our full potential. They helped me understand how having optimal health gives us the energy we need to fulfill our Divine purpose. They helped me understand that I needed to include health in this book because, without it, we cannot live our purposefully, create prosperity, or passionate relationships.

It was through this discovery that I also realized other women felt this calling to lift and support others in having optimal health. I realized that not only could I support them with doing that by sharing free coaching, and the entire system I use in my own business, but that I could literally link arms with these incredible women.

We could create a team of people who genuinely care about others, who are passionate about health, and who are motivated to walk alongside them, coaching and supporting them as they built their business.

If you would like to get more information about joining our team, reach out to a Fire Within Coach for a free discovery call at www.myfirewithin.com/resources.

Digging Deep
What is one new healthy habit you can do daily?

How would improving your health help you to feel better physically, emotionally, spiritually, and in all the relationships in your life?

If you would like support with taking the next step toward your health goals, book a discovery call with a Fire Within Coach at www.myfirewithin.com/resources.

SECTION 5:
LIGHT YOUR LIFE

CHAPTER 14:
CREATING YOUR FIRE WITHIN PLAN

"The most effective way to do it is to do it." ~Amelia Earhart

YOU ARE AMAZING! You have read through this book and have all the tools that you need to be a Woman With Fire. Now it is time to put all of those things you have learned into action and make a plan to create your life with fire.

Before we get into supporting you with your Fire Within Plan, let's review what we have covered so far. In this book, we have talked about these main points:

- You have a Divine Purpose
- The Four Primary Laws of Fire help you align with your Divine Purpose.

    - The Four Primary Laws of Fire are State, Alignment, Service, Growth.

- F.I.R.E. Priorities help us to stay in priority.

    - They are (First you, Inspiration, Relationship with your partner, Engage with kids.

- F.I.R.E. Goals help us to achieve goals predictably

    - F.I.R.E. Goals are Focus, Incentive, Responsible, Exact time

- Seasons with F.I.R.E. helps us to stay in priority & reach our goals, no matter what is going on in life.

    - Seasons with F.I.R.E. are Flexible, Inspired Action, Relationships, Expectations

- Creating a Prosperous Future involves growing your money tree
- Creating passionate relationships is all about the bond

Now that we have reviewed some of the main ideas we have covered in this book, we are ready to move on to support you in creating your own Fire Within Plan. In creating your plan, you are going to take a look at your life as it is now and the life that you want to create. Think about where you are in the following areas of your life: physically, socially, spiritually, and intellectually. We need to pay attention to and be growing in each of these areas throughout our lives. All of these areas are interconnected, and all of them are connected to the Four Primary Laws of Fire.

Taking care of our physical health aligns with the Primary Law of State of Mind. It allows us to have the energy and the physical, financial, and emotional resources we need to accomplish our goals.

The Primary Law of Alignment is addressed through our spiritual goals. These are critical to staying connected with the Creator and receiving Divine inspiration.

Being socially connected aligns with the Primary Law of Service. When we are connected to and serving others, we feel like we belong. This helps us to both give and receive support.

Being inspired and stretching ourselves intellectually, addresses the Primary Law of Growth. It helps us to grow our belief in what is possible and expand our capacity to serve others and ourselves.

I love that when we choose one goal in each of these areas, we automatically enact the power of the Four Primary Laws of Fire. We are strengthening our capacity and character and are striving to create more of the life we are destined for.

What is one goal you could strive for in each of these areas; physical, spiritual, intellectual, and social? Using F.I.R.E. goals, how could you set and achieve one or more of these goals?

And why is it important for you to make these changes in your life?

After you answer that question and before we dive into creating a plan, we need to stop for a moment and reflect on your journey so far. Reflection is how we can squeeze the juice out of the things you have learned. So, what is your biggest lesson? What principles in this book will make your life even better?

What is one area of your life that is most important to you to make even better? Is it having more secure finances, more passionate and loving relationships, starting or growing your business, feeling more connected to the Divine?

Whatever it is, get clear on the one thing that would make your life even more incredible. The one thing that is most important to you.

Now, what is your very next step to creating that change that is most important to you? Remember, it does not have to be a giant leap; it just needs to be a small step. As an ancient American Native person named Alma said, "It is with small things that great things come to pass."

To begin on your path to greatness, we need to know what the next step is.

Get down to your big why by asking yourself *why is making these changes so important to me?* Then continue to ask yourself why until you get down to your big why. This is the way that is going to drive you through all the muck of every day when you lose motivation when it feels too hard when you forget why you are doing it. This big why is what you are going to hold onto to keep a remembrance of the life you are fighting for.

The life that stretches your comfort zone and what you believe is possible and takes more work than you thought it would, but then at the end of it, the reward is worth it.

I know how important it is to have support in reaching our goals.

If you would like support creating your own Fire Within Plan, go to www.myfirewithin.com/resources to book your free discovery call.

Creating the life you want rather than the one you feel like you should have, or the one you feel like everyone else thinks you should have is so worth it. You are on a journey of discovery that is going to take you to the highest mountains of your soul and sometimes to the darkest depths, but the struggle and fight that you go through will make you stronger, more capable of overcoming anything and you will get clearer about what you are fighting for.

I know that in the thick of life, we can easily get lost and can sometimes lose sight of what is most important. Being clear about your goals and taking consistent small steps toward them will help you achieve the results you want.

All you need to do next is take action on creating the life you want, one step at a time.

Get Support

You have embarked on this incredible journey, and you have all the tools you need to succeed, but you don't have to do it alone!

There is an entire community of women just like you who are working on creating their abundant life right along with you. You can easily connect with these women through the My Fire Within Facebook Group.

The thing I love most about women is that we support each other. There is an incredible power that comes from women working together towards a common goal with an attitude of acceptance, love, and community. Together we truly can do great things. Join us and get the support you need to take your life to the next level and, through your experiences, lift and inspire others.

When we have successes in different areas of our life, it becomes our responsibility to help others to create the life they want. Who is someone you know who needs this message of hope, encouragement, and love? Who is someone in your life who is feeling stuck or feeling like they are not living up their potential or who wants more out of life?

I am very aware that you are on this journey for a reason and that you picked up this book for a reason. You are the only person in this world who can reach out and serve the people around you. You are put in contact with the people you know and love to help them. How can you help share this knowledge with them so they can create the life they want?

Being a Woman with Fire

First of all, I need to tell you how incredible I think you are and how much respect I have for you!

Your finishing this book tells me a lot about you. You are someone who is committed to creating an inspired life that is filled with purpose, prosperity, and passion. You are someone who is not willing to settle for mediocrity. You are a woman who is willing to fight against all the odds to create the life you dream of. You are committed to living your purpose by using the talents and skills you have. You are someone who is not willing to sacrifice your family to get to your goals. You are a woman who is courageous, strong, determined, and unstoppable. You are truly incredible!

Now you have a choice to make. Are you going to apply these principles in your daily life? It would be easy to read this book and dismiss the message or procrastinate on implementing the principles revealed.

You are standing on your own edge right now—an edge of knowing for yourself that these principles are true. Only you can take this step. I have taken you as far as I can. Now you need to take what you have learned and move forward with faith, knowing that you have it within you to create an inspired and incredible life.

There will be times in your journey on this path when things get tough, and when you don't feel like you have it in you. When you feel like giving up. Don't give up! Know that it is normal to have these challenges along the path.

You don't have to be perfect; you don't have to be graceful; you just need to take the next step. The time is now for you to begin this journey of unleashing your fire. Take that step forward toward a life that is more incredible than you can imagine.

As you take that step, know that you are not alone. The Creator knows you and loves you and will be there with you through it all. That doesn't mean this path won't be difficult at times, but it will always be worth it.

As you align with the principles you learned in this book, you will be lifted and strengthened. You will receive the many miraculous results that come from living true principles. As you live your purpose and use your talents to help the people around you, you will unleash a part of yourself more powerful than you know. You will be on the Creator's errand, and He will be there with you every step of the way.

I have truly loved being here with you throughout this journey. I am grateful for your willingness to learn, your courage to move forward, and your commitment to an inspired life. I think you are phenomenal, and I would love to hear your story about how these principles have helped you and how you are living a purposeful and passionate life. My greatest joy is seeing other women create the life they desire and change the world by changing themselves.

You are now part of a group of women who know we don't need to choose between our families and making a difference in the world. We seek divine inspiration, take courageous action to live our purpose, increase our prosperity, and uplift others.

Stand back and take notice world, we are Women With Fire!